May 1, 2020

M000103960

To Joe,

Wishing you great
success in all your
current and future
endeavors.

Philippe Bouisson

Additional praise for

ALIGNING THE DOTS

Engaging, profound and thought-provoking, Philippe Bouissou is so passionate about relating strategy to growth to execution. *Aligning the Dots* illustrates the science he is bringing to these relationships.

BRACKEN DARRELL
CEO of Logitech

A captivating read introducing new principles for successfully growing any company.

GORDON SEGAL
Founder and former CEO of Crate and Barrel

Transformative and brilliantly constructed. *Aligning the Dots* is an extraordinary journey into the world of top-line growth. The stories are captivating, the methodology is insightful and the results impressive. I wish I had read this book decades ago. I highly recommend it.

SHELLYE ARCHAMBEAU
Board member at Verizon and Nordstrom, former CEO of MetricStream

Philippe Bouissou provides a powerful and inspiring roadmap for accelerating the growth of your business. His alignment framework will help countless companies and leaders. Truly worth reading and applying!

HUBERT JOLY
Executive Chairman and former CEO of Best Buy

Bouissou is one of the smartest guys in the Valley. His groundbreaking framework to understand and drive GROWTH will produce supercharged results.

RANDY CHESLER
President and CEO of Glacier Bancorp

The growth methodology introduced in *Aligning the Dots* is a concise yet powerful way to drive growth by aligning your business' products and services to address customers' pain points and delight them. Very insightful and pragmatic book by Dr. Bouissou.

LIP-BU TAN
CEO of Cadence Design Systems, Chairman of Walden International

Bouissou's background as a successful entrepreneur, first-class investor and theoretical physicist enabled him to come up with a powerful methodology for growth. To be read and applied by any CEO, General Manager or business owner.

PASCAL CAGNI
Founder and CEO of C4 Ventures, former General Manager of Apple Europe

●● Genius often creates out-of-the-box thinking. *Aligning the Dots* makes you think differently and that makes it powerful. Any business should understand and use these concepts.

NOLAN BUSHNELL
CEO of X2 Games,
founder and former CEO of Atari and Chuck E Cheese!

●● *Aligning the Dots* is essential for CEOs to grow their business. It's a brutal reminder to measure relative market share and align your business plans based on it, lest perish. Philippe offer compelling examples from which to learn.

RAY LANE
Managing Partner, Greatpoint Ventures, former President, Oracle Corporation,
former Chairman of Hewlett Packard and Carnegie Mellon University

●● *Aligning the Dots* provides powerful rules and principles for growth: understand what market you want to go after, obsessively align your offering to that market and make sure your stakeholders are also aligned internally behind a purpose and a strong set of values. As a former CEO of a global brand, now backing startups in seed stage, I totally connected with the content of the book. It is truly an inspiring read for all who are motivated to grow their business.

ODILE ROUJOL
Founder of Fab Ventures,
former CEO and President, Lancôme International (L'Oréal)

●● Philippe Bouissou's methodology of external alignment on four axes, coupled with internal alignment, for me, is unique, transformative and consequential. It will be recognized as such in the world of business literature similarly to Michael Porter's book, *Competitive Strategy*. I would advise any business leader, CEO, entrepreneur, business owner, board member or investor to read it and learn from it.

JOHN DEAN
President and CEO of Central Pacific Bank,
former Chairman and CEO of Silicon Valley Bank

●● While *Aligning the Dots* won't make it magically easy, Bouissou's *A4 Precision Alignment*™ methodology and compelling case studies will help you avoid the critical misalignments that keep many companies from achieving their full growth potential.

DRUE FREEMAN
CEO of ACG (Association for Corporate Growth) Silicon Valley

●● An insightful and valuable read. Leaders from the boardroom right down who are committed to growth will benefit immensely from the powerful approach and pragmatic suggestions made throughout this book.

ANITA SANDS, Ph.D.
Board member at ServiceNow, Symantec, Pure Storage and ThoughtWorks

ALIGNING
THE
DOTS

ONWARD BUSINESS PRESS
Palo Alto, California

ALIGNING
THE
DOTS

**The new paradigm
to grow any
business**

Philippe Bouissou, Ph.D.

ALIGNING THE DOTS: THE NEW PARADIGM TO GROW ANY BUSINESS

Published by

ONWARD BUSINESS PRESS

Photograph and Art Credits

Page 2: Copyright Tom Fishburne, marketoonist.com and reproduced by permission of Marketoonist
Page 21: Picture by Jon Devore reproduced by permission of Luke Aikins
Page 22: Courtesy of National Aeronautics and Space Administration
Page 24: LIGO Livingston, courtesy of Caltech/MIT/LIGO Laboratory
Page 26: Courtesy of Hanayama reproduced by permission of Teddy Sakamoto

Publishing advisor: Karla Olson
Editors: Elaine Cummings and Lisa Wolff
Proofreader: Sara Hunt
Indexer: Ken DellaPenta
Book designer: Charles McStravick

ISBN: 978-1-7342087-0-2
ISBN (eBook): 978-1-7342087-1-9

Library of Congress Control Number: 2019917903

www.PhilippeBouissou.com

This book may be purchased in bulk for promotional, educational, or business use.
Please inquire at the author website above.

PRINTED IN THE UNITED STATES OF AMERICA

To all who aspire
to grow their business,
small or big.

How well is your business aligned for growth?

Getting your business aligned, internally and externally,
is essential for growth.

Are you ready to take your business to the next level?
If you are a CEO, a GM of a business unit or responsible for a P&L,
take ten minutes to answer a dozen questions. Point your browser to:

☞   www.PhilippeBouissou.com

You will receive a free, customized and confidential report
that will show your *Business Alignment Score*™
and identify areas you should focus on
to start growing your business.

It only takes **10** minutes...

CONTENTS

HOW TO READ THIS BOOK

By highlighting new ideas, unique concepts and pragmatic tools that are fundamentally useful, I designed this book to have both immediate and lasting impact and value.

I know that time is one of your greatest assets. You're busy and your mind is in overdrive. I'm guessing you find yourself preoccupied with needs and ideas big and small, significant and futile, pressing and long term. I've been in your shoes (and most days, I'm still there!). So, I organized this book in a different way. It's written so that you can maximize the return on the time you invest in it. Skip around and read in a non-linear fashion if that suits you. Or read it cover-to-cover.

However you choose to engage with the content, here are some suggestions:

IF YOU HAVE ...	... THEN
3 minutes	Pique your curiosity by reading just the summary on page 197.
10 minutes	Let me plant some seeds as you read the summary section at the end of each chapter that highlights what we've learned and relevant case studies.
30 minutes	Pick one or two relevant chapters.
more time or can't fall asleep	You'll derive the maximum value by reading *Aligning the Dots* cover-to-cover.

I'd love to hear from you. If you want to share any comments or suggest how I can improve the usefulness of the book, please reach out to me at:

☞ www.PhilippeBouissou.com

"

Success is a lousy teacher.
It seduces smart people into
thinking they can't lose.

BILL GATES
Co-chair, Bill & Melinda Gates Foundation

WHY YOU SHOULD READ THIS BOOK

In my 30 years of starting, running and investing in Silicon Valley businesses, one of the most painful and meaningful lessons I learned is that when a business is not growing relative to its market, it's on a declining path. Losing market share is never good, especially when it's to the point where the business becomes immaterial and slips to a slow death. In some ways, irrelevancy can be worse than death, dragging on for a long time. It's a little like playing Monopoly when the board is filled with houses and hotels, but none of them are yours. You know there is no way you will win, and your friends are getting richer and richer by the minute. It's the slow spiral down to irrelevancy, and eventually, game over.

For entrepreneurs, founders or CEOs who have sold shares to raise money, growing their business faster than the market in which it operates is the key to sustainable shareholder value creation. You would think that CEOs, business owners, executive management, investors, advisors and board members would have access to a pragmatic, data-driven and actionable playbook with a roadmap to outperforming their target market.

Surprisingly, in more cases than not, that blueprint does not exist.

There are volumes of literature about listening, managing and supporting your customers, marketing techniques, the art of hiring and retaining talented individuals, building a strong and lasting culture, having the right product/market fit, training and developing effective compensation plans for your salesforce, managing your time and your team as a business leader, dealing with a difficult board of directors, and of course, embracing and driving innovation. While most of these concepts and ideas are sensible, there is no disciplined, data-driven and universal approach to top-line growth.

As a CEO, I often struggled with that deceptively simple question: "What should I do on Monday morning at eight o'clock to grow my business faster than our target market and faster than my competitors?"

The search for a clear answer led me to this body of work. *A4 Precision Alignment*™ is a new paradigm—a rigorous, commonsense and data-driven approach to solving the revenue growth problem. This is not your traditional business book with concepts you have heard before. My goal is to empower you to look at the world from a fundamentally new prospective based on the profound notion of *alignment*. Dozens of examples, case studies and specific data models demonstrate how to realize the perfect alignment for your business and inform actions that can unleash extraordinary revenue growth potential.

I hope you enjoy the journey. If there is something, just a little something, that makes you look at the challenge of growing your business differently, then I have accomplished my mission. You will have helped me achieve my humble definition of success and made every hour I spent thinking about the topic of growth and authoring this book worthwhile. And for that, you have my deepest gratitude.

Philippe Bouissou, Ph.D.
Palo Alto, California

"

There is only growth or death.

BRACKEN DARRELL
CEO of Logitech

THE GROWTH IMPERATIVE

The thing about growth

Growth is at the core of our very existence. It is deeply embedded in our DNA. Can you imagine the world with children never growing into adulthood? A plant that never grew? What if our knowledge remained stagnant? Our planet and world would be quite different. It would not have any life on it.

Our own universe is growing. In fact, recent data from the Hubble Space Telescope shows that the universe is expanding faster than we thought. Using the space telescope, astrophysicists measure distances to other galaxies by examining a certain type of star, called a Cepheid variable, that varies in brightness. Imagine if the Big Bang had not existed. That's obviously hard, since we would not exist and would not be reading these words.

In the business world where markets are rapidly changing, top-line growth is also imperative for survival. New contenders are relentlessly entering the race, innovation and technology shakes the status quo, and new business models are invented. Savvier consumers demand more value from the goods and services they consume and want to enjoy exciting new user experiences. In this environment, a company that is not growing is on a slow decline to irrelevancy. Growth becomes a practical matter of life and death[1].

The dilemma of the status quo

For most businesses, growth is the engine of shareholder value creation. Mathematically, a business that is not growing faster than the market in which it operates is losing market share and is letting its competition seize revenue. Market-leading companies command a much larger share of value compared to their share of market and are therefore disproportionately rewarded. The largest companies in the world by market value could not have reached their leading positions if they had not grown faster than their respective market. That's the only way to get to the top. Chris Zook and James Allen in their well-researched book *Profit from the Core* rightfully so observe:

> 66 The average sustained value creator in our database grew twice as rapidly as its industry in revenue...

---

1   There are many small businesses that structurally can't or don't need to grow, yet their survival depends on their ability to adapt to market changes. Their goal is to generate a predictable cash flow. They tend to be lifestyle businesses. Examples would be farming businesses, dentist practices, small gardening/yard-servicing companies, solo-practitioner consultants, pet services, family-owned restaurants, small divorce attorney practices, mechanic shops, and many others.

Conversely, shareholder value decreases when companies lose market share. According to Bain and Company, only one out of ten companies are able to maintain profitable growth, even at a modest level, over a period of ten years. The winners are the ones that exhibit consistent, sustainable steady growth relative to their markets. They provide greater returns in the long run than precipitous hyper-growth examples. These are the 10X companies Jim Collins describes so well in his book *Great by Choice*.

If you were to read the death certificate of a company, you would see something along these lines: "Company ran out of money and had to cease operations." I have heard many times from my VC colleagues and others that companies die because they run out of cash. I don't subscribe to this way of thinking. It's a little like saying people die because their heart stopped. Surely at some point their heart stopped beating, but this is not the cause of death in medical terms. The real question is: Why did their heart stop? Did they succumb to lung cancer? Were they hit by a car and suffered massive head trauma that caused uncontrollable bleeding in their brain? Was it a pulmonary embolism? Lack of top-line growth is really what should be written on the company's death certificate, not cash deprivation. The problem is loss of revenue momentum. When expenses are managed and revenue is there, a mature company will reach profitability and generate cash. As long as cash is generated, the company goes on and can live for a long time.

You may wonder, "What about profits?" The temptation of a newly appointed CEO might be to cut costs or, put in more euphemistic terms, "manage expenses." Most of the time, it creates shareholder value as the earnings per share (EPS) goes up. But it's not sustainable. Once Wall Street has considered the increase in EPS and factored it into the company's valuation, additional shareholder value will need to be generated from somewhere else. From where, then? The answer is to grow the top line faster than the market, gaining market share to build a more dominant position.

High revenue growth generates higher valuation than the growth of profits. The fundamental reason is that there is an inherent limit to the level of profitability that can be achieved and therefore a limit to its growth. A company cannot exceed its top-line revenue in profits. In an ultimate and unrealistic scenario, a company generating $100 million in revenue with zero expenses would generate $100 million in profit. Of course, this is a hypothetical case assuming a business with 100% gross margins and no fixed expenses, no cost of sales, no marketing or R&D or administrative expenses, and no cost of management and support. This scenario does not exist. The point is that profitability is always capped; it cannot be larger than the top line. In that sense, the bottom line is always the slave to the top line. Even if the gross margin percentage stays constant or even decreases slightly, if the top-line growth is significant, then there is still more and more money to cover fixed costs and investments. It also covers a lot of the sins of operational misses.

On the other hand, **there is no limit to the top line.** Amazon is a stunning example of a company going through the roof: it grew from $0 to $233 billion in 25 years.

Top-line growth is also critical for mid- to late-stage venture capital (VC) and most private equity (PE)–backed companies[2]. At the moment the first share of a company is sold to an investor, the job of the CEO has been irreversibly altered. That transaction fundamentally redefines the game. It's a subtle, sometimes unnoticed, but profound effect. It puts the company on a different trajectory. The quid pro quo for taking money now forces the CEO to run and lead the company to build sustainable shareholder value, and that can only happen if and when the company grows faster than its target market. Lack of revenue growth is really how the death certificates should read for most VC- and many PE-backed companies, as opposed to cash deprivation. This is because **revenue growth enables CEOs to raise more capital, hire talented people, acquire other companies and ultimately generate cash flow.**

There is little doubt that a company that is struggling to grow would have a hard time attracting VC or PE investors. In its *Annual Global PE Deal Multiples* report for 2018, PitchBook shared the results of its quarterly survey of PE respondents who completed at least one financial transaction during the quarter the survey was conducted. One of the most interesting takeaways is that PE firms tend not to invest in companies with decreased trailing 12-month revenue. In fact, in 2018, 68% of the investments were made in companies with projected revenue growth above 10% in the next 12 months.

2　A notable exception is Danaher, which buys large properties that can be made more profitable by shoring up business processes. Danaher may only expect low single-digit growth, but with significant bottom-line improvement. Cerberus invests in large distressed properties and "fixes" the operations of the business, oftentimes increasing value via EBITDA multiples rather than top-line revival. Different PE firms have different strategies. However non-seed VCs, by definition, are growth mongers.

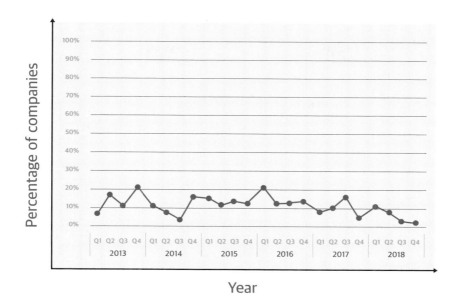

Percentage of PE investment in companies with decreasing revenue over 12 months prior to deal

The number of cases where the PE firms invested in companies with revenue decreasing 12 months prior to making the investment averaged 12%. In other words, if your company is not growing its top line, it is very hard to convince a PE firm to invest in it.

In April 2014, McKinsey published an article entitled "Grow Fast or Die Slow" based on research on 3,000 software and online services companies and their business cycles between 1980 and 2012. Key insights from the article shed light on the following:

- High growth generates significantly better shareholder value (five times more) compared to medium-growth companies.

- Success can be predicted by growth: companies with growth over 60% at the time they reached $100 million in revenue were eight times more likely to reach $1 billion in revenue compared to those growing at less than 20%.

- Growth matters more than margin or cost structure in terms of shareholder value creation.

- Sustaining growth is hard: 85% of the high-growth companies did not maintain their growth rate of at least 60%.

From seed to maturity: the five stages of business growth

A while ago, a woman in a park asked me, "How old is your dog?" I answered tongue-in-cheek, "Thirty-five years." The dubious woman said, laughing, "He does not look that old!" Of course, I was talking human years. Our dog, Rio, a lovely Havanese, was five years old at the time.

What about the age of a company? If you multiply the age of a dog by seven to find the equivalent age in human years, what do you use for a company? I found out that multiplying by three, determining the age of a company works well. It typically takes somewhere around seven years for a startup to enjoy a "liquidity event" as we say in the VC business, i.e. be acquired or go public. That's like being 21 years old. Going public at that age is like being legally allowed to drink alcohol. If you drink too much and don't follow the rules, you pay a high price. Same for a company that misses its first-quarter estimate after going public.

Human beings move from birth to end of life through different phases of growth. It is well established that there are five phases to this process:

1. Infancy (birth to about one year old/walking)
2. Early childhood (two to five years)
3. Middle childhood, also known as prepubescence (six to 11 years)
4. Adolescence (12 to 18 years)
5. Adulthood

In a similar way, companies also go through five different stages of growth throughout their business lifecycle:

1. **SEED:** The company is at a concept and development phase of the product: no revenue is generated. This is the phase where ideas are turned into a product.

2. **NURTURING OR STARTUP PHASE:** First revenue/sales to customers; usually driven by the founders or CEO. The goal is to see if the market responds and to keep going and "live another month." The company earns the right to go to the next phase. It should be noted that the choice of these initial customers is also

important. Emphasis should to be put on market segmentation. Focus on customers who will positively influence the next version of the product and will be solid reference customers and advocates. Some call them "Shaping Customers."[3]

3. **ADOLESCENCE:** This is the market insertion stage, when revenue starts to grow in a more predictable way. In this phase, market resonance happens, and discipline is brought to the sales process. Skilled employees are hired, and a support infrastructure for sales, marketing and customer care is put in place. This is about survival and "living another year." The owner or CEO continues to be synonymous with the business at that stage; he/she *is* the business.

4. **EXPANSION:** At this stage, running the business is well understood and the sales flywheel is turning with a decent level of predictability. The company ventures into new and unknown territories such as geographic expansion, new product lines, establishing distribution and channel partners, first acquisition and upgraded board of directors. It is the transition from a single product, channel and market to multiple products, channels and markets. This is the phase where the notion of granularity (business units) is introduced to support the rapid growth. The owner, founder or CEO may not be the best person to drive that expansion anymore. VCs often consider bringing an "adult" CEO and an experienced CFO during that phase, with founders focusing on what they were best at during the early stage of the company (product development, technology, marketing or sales). Attention moves to the future of the business rather than its current state.

5. **MATURITY:** Profits and cash flow are now generated by a well-oiled machine. Growth rates typically slow down at this phase. Controls, strategic and operations planning, and processes have to be in place to be successful during this phase of the business. Systems (finance, HR, IT, CRM, client success, ticketing for support, product development and product release and just as importantly, talent management) are now well established. Executives understand and apply operational and strategic planning in a decentralized organization. Delegation is not an afterthought, but a must-do. Now company size, financial well-being and

---

3   This term came up during a discussion I had with Lip-Bu Tan, the CEO of Cadence Design Systems, a $2 billion revenue company focused on electronic design systems.

management talent can be leveraged for a great exit or a "take no prisoners" acquisitive approach. This is a dangerous phase, where innovation and entrepreneurship can easily get squashed and politics moves into high gear. The company must engineer its second act and find the next S-curve that will bring a new wave of growth beyond the original business.

Arie de Geus's work on the "living company" suggested that the average life expectancy of corporations in the Northern Hemisphere is well under 20 years. Only those who are able to expand after surviving high-risk infancy continue to live another 20 to 30 years. (Source: *Harvard Business Review,* March–April 1997, 23.)

Here is a rough attempt to map the five phases of company growth to a revenue number:

STAGE	👤 HUMAN BEING		🛡 COMPANY	
1	Infancy	Birth to ~1 year (walking)	Seed	No revenue (inception to about 1 year)
2	Early Childhood	2 to 5 years	Nurturing	$1 to $1M (1 to 2 years)
3	Middle Childhood	6 to 11 years	Adolescence	$1 to $10M (2 to 4 years)
4	Adolescence	12 to 18 years	Expansion	$1 to $100M (3 to 6 years)
5	Adulthood[4]	Over 18	Maturity	$100M (after ~6 years)

Growth phases of human beings and companies

4 Adulthood is split in three phases: young adulthood from 18 to 39 years, middle adulthood from 40 to 60 years and elder/senior citizenship when over 60 years old.

As the company goes from birth to adulthood, revenue typically follows an S-curve:

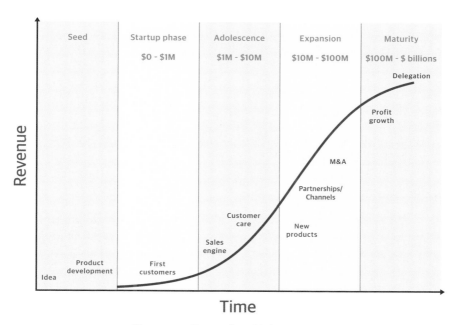

The revenue S-curve from birth to maturity

For a company to grow from no revenue to billions of dollars of revenue, it will have to travel through these five stages in its lifecycle.

Growing is like drinking: it needs to be done responsibly

I believe that the venture capital industry, particularly in Silicon Valley, has been doing a disservice to many entrepreneurs lately. Investors have been aggressively pushing their CEOs and management teams to grow at unsustainable rates to attract new investors so that they can pour in more and more capital, hoping that the company continues to sustain an unreasonable growth rate. This vicious cycle has been detrimental and continues to hurt entrepreneurs, forcing them to grow for the sake of growth or grow at all costs, in order to justify unreasonably higher and higher valuations. Additional capital dilutes employee ownership and raises the bar for employees to make money from their stock options because of artificially inflated valuations and punishing liquidation preferences. It is not unusual now to see rounds of financing in the hundreds of millions of dollars and even in the billion-dollar range. Uber and SoftBank are the poster children for this exuberance.

In order to sustain these growth rates, management teams have to cut too many corners. Unit economics are forgotten, and the line-of-sight to profitability is so blurry that no one pays attention to it. It is certainly not top-of-mind, and in many cases, not even in the picture. Profitability has become exceedingly rare for companies going public, in the name of insane growth to win the horse race. Lyft's IPO prospectus is telling. It reads: "We have a history of net losses and we may not be able to achieve or maintain profitability in the future." Recruiting, training and retaining hundreds of new employees in a very short period of time is a massive challenge that threatens the wellness of the culture and the very DNA of the company. During hyper-growth, it is very difficult to onboard the right talent fast enough to support demand. This leads to dilution of tribal knowledge and raises the likelihood that old mistakes will be repeated, but with much greater impact. Business infrastructure, fiscal responsibility, business planning, processes, progress tracking and disciplined execution become an afterthought. This is unreasonable growth that only works in some very rare, but unfortunately well publicized, cases.

For most companies, it is very difficult to maintain a high growth rate. Growth does not last forever. A 2012 study done by Andy Vitus, partner at Scale Venture Partners, shows that next year's growth rate is likely to be 85% of this year's growth rate for recurring-revenue companies. In other words, growth rates tend to naturally decay. The dataset covers more than 60 companies ranging from $1 million to $1 billion in sales with growth rates between 10% and 120% (very few rules seem to apply outside these parameters).

Some VC-backed companies, in order to maintain a high growth rate, waste a lot of money on marketing and sales and hiring the wrong people. Reed Taussig, a successful CEO with a great track record, explained to me that throwing salespeople at the problem is rarely the answer. The issue is not the supply, it's demand. He was asked by some of his investors to look at the effect of additional revenue when the sales and marketing budget is increased by 50%. It turned out that only 22% of companies saw a large increase, 10% saw a modest one, 33% saw their revenue decline and the rest were essentially flat. Instead, the CEO should focus on truly understanding the CAC (customer acquisition cost) and find the right go-to-market strategy that supports a low enough CAC to reach profitability. It is fine to stay on the edge of growth, but don't get ahead of yourself in terms of spending and recruiting. This will give you freedom and sustainable power. It also forces you to be focused. **Once you see the opportunity to grow, then you can scale at a responsible rate.**

High growth cannot and should not be considered in a vacuum. It is usually pursued to the detriment of something else. It always has to be balanced and is always a trade-off. Identifying and being aware of that trade-off is a really important step before deciding to execute the right growth strategy. **The more aggressive the pursuit of growth, the more impact it will have on other aspects of the business.**

It is similar to the Heisenberg principle (also known as the "Uncertainty Principle") in physics. In 1927, German physicist Werner Heisenberg stated that the position and the velocity of a particle couldn't both be measured in an exact manner, at the same time, even in theory. This was a disconcerting revelation that puzzled many physicists for a long time. Another way to think about it is that the more precise the measurement of, say, the position of a particle, the less precisely its velocity can be determined. You have to choose one to the exclusion of the other in terms of accurate determination.

So, the key question is: If I aggressively grow, how much will it be to the detriment of my business? What other parts of the organization will it affect and how? What price will I have to ultimately pay? The paradox is that the quest for higher growth can create a situation where growth becomes inhibited. This is because there are some inherent and intrinsic limits to how fast any business can grow. **These limits and boundaries must be well understood and respected in order to deliver what I call responsible growth.**

Here are some examples of possible impediments to growth:

- Challenge to recruit, onboard and manage quality talent
- Company culture is weak or eroding
- Low employee morale and retention
- Insufficient required capital to execute
- Low gross margins and profitability
- Inconsistent product quality
- Deteriorating service levels
- Inability to control the message
- Creating unnecessary stress to the organization
- Channel partners unable to execute
- Customer confusion vis-à-vis the product offering (too many products or overly complicated choices)
- Overall loss of focus

Growth at all costs does not work in the long run and can lead to a disastrous situation. High growth does not last forever and management teams, board members and investors need to be prepared for it.

CRATE AND BARREL

Growing while preserving its DNA

A good example of responsible growth is the case of Crate and Barrel. In December 2017, I had the privilege and honor to speak with Gordon Segal, its founder and former CEO. He told me his fascinating story.

Over half a century ago, on December 7, 1962, Segal and his wife, Carole, opened their first Crate and Barrel store in an abandoned elevator factory in Chicago's Old Town district. The idea came to them after their honeymoon in the Caribbean islands where they found small stores carrying Scandinavian-designed products at very reasonable prices. With limited resources and a sense of adventure, creativity kicked in, and the pinewood crates and the barrels in which the various products where shipped from Europe were used to display items for sale. Several days before opening, a friend who was visiting the store suggested they name the new business "Barrel and Crate," but Carole preferred "Crate and Barrel."

The first year was hard and was managed on a shoestring budget. Gordon and Carole visited Europe to scout producers and factories to uncover appealing and well-designed products and began buying directly from them, bypassing the wholesalers. The first new large store opened in 1965, and fours year later they bought a furniture store in Cambridge, Massachusetts.

Crate and Barrel now sells a large variety of housewares, home furnishings and furniture. One of the key innovations was to display items in a configuration similar to how they would be in the comfort of a home.

Preserving a solid culture and a high standard of product design and quality were dictating the rules of growth for the company. Growth in and of itself was never the goal or the endgame for Gordon and Carole, although it was important. They loved merchandising more. During the 40 years Gordon ran the company, there had been only one year where the top line did not grow.

In 1998, the Otto Group, a German company and the largest direct marketing company in Europe, bought two-thirds of the company. The transaction helped bring liquidity to the company and its owners and provided personal financial upside to its key associates. At age 70, Gordon stepped down as the CEO and promoted Barbara Turf, his head collaborator and head merchant, to take the helm. She had first joined the company as a sales associate in 1965. At the time of Gordon's retirement, the company was doing over $1.1 billion in sales, had over 100 stores and had 7,000 employees.

When I talked to Gordon about growth, he shared with me the secret for success that has never changed over 50 years: create and foster an environment for consumers to discover and buy beautifully designed housewares and furniture. By sourcing these products directly, originally from Europe and then worldwide, the middleman or wholesaler was eliminated and consequently, the products could be sold at a more reasonable price. For example, if a manufacturer sold the product to the distributor for $10, the distributor would sell it to a retailer for $18, who would then sell it to the consumer for $40. Gordon's idea was to buy directly from the manufacturer, so the product could now be sold for $20 to $25, at a significant discount to the end consumer.

Maintaining a strong culture of mutual respect, aesthetics, design, quality and exciting merchandising was one of the most important and difficult endeavors. A great deal of time was spent developing associates. This deliberate home-grown process imposed a slower, yet more controlled growth. A strong work ethic, a good sense of humor, caring and the drive to educate their associates to guide consumers were the foundations of the company's DNA. The Operations were of course the engine of the business: buying, warehousing, inventory management, logistics and shipping. But it was the commitment to treating employees, suppliers and vendors with loyalty and respect that gained the firm long-term relationships with vendors, associates and customers.

When the organization seriously entered the furniture business in 1989/1990 with three very large stores in Chicago, significant investments were made to insure fast delivery of furniture (92% of sales were delivered within a week). The business soon boomed as the same philosophy that was used to grow housewares was applied to furniture. Over the next 20 years, all of the Crate and Barrel housewares stores were converted to stores selling both housewares and furniture, tripling the average square footage of these stores.

In the late 1990s, when one of the weaknesses of the company was direct mail and their major competitor, Williams-Sonoma, which was founded six years before Crate and Barrel, was doing half of their business in-store and half though their mailing catalogs, the Segals decided that partnering with the Otto Group, Europe's largest direct marketer, would be a good strategic fit. It proved to be a very good decision and as a result, internet sales now drive a large portion of the Crate and Barrel business.

According to Gordon, the key ingredients of success and growth were:

- Delivering a new experience by bringing curated, beautiful, tasteful and quality-designed products from Scandinavia and Europe to American homes at a fair price;

- Building a solid operational infrastructure to support the buying experience and the flow of goods; and

- Developing and engaging in a company culture of high ethical behavior and caring for its associates, who in turn would care for and respect their customers.

By having no other shareholders in the beginning, Gordon and his team could pace their growth in a measured way to maintain these key success factors. While growth was important, their ideals were never compromised. It was driven more by the idea of slow, careful growth, so the emphasis could be on great merchandise and superior customer service.

There are certain types of industries like retail and restaurants (not chain restaurants) that have an intrinsic limitation to growth in order for the DNA to be replicated and preserved.

Consistency is critical to success. These kinds of industries tend to grow at their own intrinsic rate, store by store. Gordon explained that it would take three years to really develop a great store manager and two years for a talented visual merchandiser. Trying to grow too fast can be the kiss of death. This is not about growing for the sake of growing. This is about spreading and preserving a unique experience, a culture and a sense of family and camaraderie.

CASE STUDY

How are growth and alignment related?

A few years ago, a key insight came to me almost by surprise. I realized that:

 The optimal growth rate of a company can only be achieved when the company is perfectly aligned with its market.

When a company starts to become misaligned with its market, friction is introduced, which negatively affects business momentum. The business machinery and the gears start to slow down and soon enough, in a subversive way, market share erodes. Customers are not buying at the same rate, are not as excited about the product and are not consuming at the same pace, because something, somewhere, got misaligned.

This insight is critical because when the market and business are aligned, then the maximum possible growth rate is achieved, which enables a market share increase and in turn, sustainable shareholder value creation. It lies at the heart of why and how companies succeed. The questions now become: How do you realize the perfect alignment? How is it defined? Can you measure it? How do you correct any misalignment in a prescriptive way? The rest of the book provides clear answers to these fundamental questions.

Now, the question is: what do I do on Monday morning at eight o'clock to realize a perfect alignment?

The rest of the book details how to realize external alignment between the company and its target market. It will provide answers to key questions such as: What does alignment mean? What is a pragmatic, realistic and prescriptive way to achieve that complex alignment? Can it be measured? How can it be changed?

I will introduce a new growth paradigm so that CEOs, management team members, advisors and board members can put together an action plan in order to know what to do on Monday morning at eight o'clock.

WHAT WE HAVE LEARNED

➤ Just like people are hard-wired for growth, top-line growth is essential for businesses to survive; growth is the engine of value creation.

➤ The most successful companies demonstrate consistent, sustainable and steady growth relative to their market.

➤ High revenue growth translates into higher valuation than profit growth. There is an inherent cap on profits but no ceiling on top-line growth.

➤ VC and PE firms are more likely to invest in companies with strong top-line revenue performance.

➤ The VC industry presents significant challenges for entrepreneurs due to pushing growth at unsustainable rates. Maintaining a high growth rate is extremely difficult for any company.

➤ Any growth strategy requires a company to make trade-offs; the more aggressive the pursuit of growth, the greater the impact on other aspects of the business such as employee recruitment and retention, product quality, customer support and overall focus.

➤ Key insight: The optimal growth rate of a company can only be achieved when the company is perfectly aligned with its market.

CASE STUDY

➤ Crate and Barrel: growing while preserving its DNA

NEXT CHAPTER

➤ Introduces the concept of alignment with examples drawn from adventure, science, technology and business.

"

If you are not willing to risk the unusual,
you will have to settle for the ordinary.

JIM ROHN
American entrepreneur and author

<blockquote>CHAPTER

2</blockquote>

ALIGNMENT

The core of everything

If I had to summarize this book in one word and one word only, it would have to be *alignment*. **Alignment is the key to maximizing revenue growth.** Alignment is to revenue growth what love is to happiness and oxygen is to life. It is necessary, vital and critical. There's no shortcut. It can't be escaped. It can't be sacrificed. It has to be addressed with respect, humility and passion.

In short:

 The optimal growth rate of a company
can only be achieved when the company
is perfectly aligned with its market.

I call it The Law of Alignment.

Alignment is at the core of achieving the best possible growth for any business, large or small, domestic or international, selling to consumers, governments or other businesses. It lies at the heart of why and how companies succeed. And it works remarkably well.

There are examples of alignment all around us. Some are natural phenomena like stellar objects aligned under the laws of astrophysics, or dunes aligned by the wind and governed by the forces in fluid dynamics.

Some people are capable of extreme precision alignment, mastering the stunning skills that enable a surgeon to maneuver a scalpel for delicate brain surgery or the pilots of the US Navy's Blue Angels F/A-18 Super Hornet fighter planes to fly in formation 18 inches apart.

Here are other attention-grabbing examples of alignment that have had a lasting effect on me.

Dying from misalignment

In July of 2015, on a hot summer day, something special happened in Ottawa, Illinois.

On their 13th attempt, 164 skydivers jumped from seven well-choreographed aircrafts at an altitude of 20,000 feet to set the record of the largest "heads down" formation. Falling at speeds of up to 240 mph, each skydiver managed to be in his or her perfect slot and hold the formation for the required minimum three seconds. Not an easy feat. You can see it on the video at www.PhilippeBouissou.com/skydive.

As a skydiver myself, I've logged 1,000 jumps and have spent more than 20 hours of my life literally free-falling at an average speed of 120 mph. So I was actually more stunned when, on February 8, 2006, nine years earlier, the news broke that in Thailand, 400 skydivers from 30 countries established the largest free-fall formation. The formation was held for more than four seconds and was logged by the Fédération Aéronautique Internationale (FAI) as the world record, which is still standing today.

In 2016, in Simi Valley, California, an amazing skydiver and experienced airplane and helicopter pilot named Luke Aikins decided to attempt a stunt called Heaven Sent that had never been purposely done before. He leaped out of a small plane flying at an altitude of 25,000 feet to accomplish the highest jump ever done without a parachute. His target was a 100 × 100-foot net. The jump lasted a mere two minutes, 120 seconds, compared to the two years it took him to meticulously prepare and train for the stunt. The remarkable video of his historic jump can be watched at www.PhilippeBouissou.com/Luke.

You see Aikins moments before he made contact with the net in the picture below:

Luke Aikins's historic skydive without a parachute on July 30, 2016

These are obviously extreme examples of precision alignment. How was each of these three world records possible?

Here's the answer: a rigorous approach, hard work and an obsession for details in the planning. Skydivers are not reckless or cavalier about jumping. We take it very seriously. Our lives are at stake. These skydivers follow sanctioned FAA rules and regulations and focused on careful safety planning, flawless execution and a never-ending quest for perfection.

Most importantly, they never could have achieved their records without a real plan and perfect alignment. These two things make the difference between success and a tragic outcome.

Precision alignment at 205 miles above the Earth

The International Space Station (ISS) is the largest object made by man, orbiting around the Earth at a low altitude of 205 miles. It carries a crew of six and can be easily seen on a clear night. Building the ISS started in 1998, and it now has circled the Earth more than 100,000 times during its almost 20 years in orbit. It weighs more than 900,000 pounds and moves at 17,000 miles per hour. The main purpose of the ISS is to conduct research in a micro-gravity environment that can't be reproduced on Earth. Research covers medicine, physics, life science, weather, material science and other scientific disciplines.

International Space Station

In order for a crew to be able to live on the ISS for long periods of time conducting research and maintenance, supplies, equipment and crew members are shuttled back and forth from Earth to the ISS. In 2018, 18 missions were on the calendar. All these missions were from the United States (Cape Kennedy or Canaveral) or Russia (Baikonur) with the exception of one from Japan.

Modules are able to rendezvous and dock. All Russian spacecraft dock fully automatically with no human intervention, using a complex system of GPS, sensors and lasers. Americans dock manually, which makes the system a lot less complex, but requires special training and makes each mission unique because of that manual process.

The person from the US team in charge of maneuvering the module into the dock is highly trained and the responsibility on his or her shoulders is immense. A small error of misalignment can be catastrophic. Imagine the challenge: you have to manually control one module flying at a speed of 17,000 miles per hour, 30 times faster than the speed of a Jumbo Jet, to find, rendezvous and then gently dock with the ISS. The orbits of the two crafts have to be the exact same, and the angles, approach speed and alignment perfectly controlled.

On June 19, 2005, there was a particularly challenging situation. Final docking commands at the ground station in Russia could not be properly uploaded to the cargo ship, necessitating a remote solution. The ISS Expedition 11 Space Station commander Sergei Krikalev, a veteran cosmonaut, had to manually dock a new cargo ship to the ISS as it was flying over Eastern Asia. The docking was a success and delivered close to 5,000 pounds of food and equipment, including some vital replacement parts for the Elektron generator, which is the primary source of oxygen that had failed the month before.

Without this perfect alignment, remote-controlled from 200 miles away by a joystick, the lives of the ISS crew would have been in serious danger and scientific space research would have suffered a great setback. In the end, human competency is always a necessary part of alignment, even when the primary aspects of an operation are automated.

The $1 billion perfect alignment

One of the most extreme exercises in alignment had perplexed scientists around the world for over 100 years. The challenge of measuring gravitational waves—the change of distance to the size of an oxygen atom ($1.2 \ 10^{-10}$ m)—was akin to measuring a baseball compared to the diameter of the Earth.

On February 11, 2016, scientists from the Laser Interferometer Gravitational-Wave Observatory (LIGO) shocked the world by announcing they had accomplished what was once believed impossible. LIGO, the largest and most ambitious project ever funded by the National Science Foundation (NSF), proved the existence of the gravitational waves. Albert Einstein predicted these waves as part of his theory of general relativity published more than a century ago. The theory specifies that space and time are warping, and as a result, ripples are created by the acceleration of massive objects in the cosmos. These waves travel throughout the universe at the speed of light and are called gravitational waves. Einstein was convinced it would never be possible to measure them.

Laser Interferometer Gravitational-Wave Observatory

The LIGO scientists registered gravitational waves that were caused by two black holes, each about 30 times as massive as our sun, that merged together over 1.3 billion years ago, which is consequential, given that the size of the known universe is about 13 billion light-years. This observation was made by two LIGO detectors separated by about 2,500 miles: one in Hanford, Washington and the other in Livingston, Louisiana. Each detector consists of two L-shaped arms that are each 2.5 miles long and perpendicular to one another. When gravitational waves hit the detector, one of the arms gets slightly elongated and the other slightly shortens. By measuring the difference in length between the two arms (1,000 times smaller than the diameter of a proton), using laser beams and interferometers, one can demonstrate the presence of gravitational waves.

David Reitze of the California Institute of Technology (Caltech), executive director of the LIGO Laboratory, describes LIGO as the most precise measuring device ever built. The first signal of wave detection was observed on September 14, 2015. The two LIGO detectors registered the two signals seven milliseconds apart. It took several months to make sure that the detection was indeed caused by gravitational waves and not polluted by the movement of Earth or another anomaly.

In 2017, shortly after the announcement of the discovery, Rainer Weiss, Barry Barish and Kip Thorne received the Nobel Prize in Physics for *decisive contributions to the LIGO detector and the observation of gravitational waves*. It had taken them 40 years of patience, frustration and tenacity to accomplish that truly remarkable feat.

It was the perfect alignment of the laser beams and complex mirror system through the interferometer that enabled the intricate LIGO detectors to work. The magnitude of the precision was almost inconceivable when the team started to work on it four decades ago. The entire project involved thousands of complex challenges. It took 55 years and a budget of $1 billion to overcome all of them. LIGO is oozing with groundbreaking technology designed specifically for the experiment. It is probably the most complex machine ever built, taking alignment to an extreme never seen before, and makes flying to the moon seem like a fifth-grade project.

Fortunately, perfectly aligning a company with its market is a lot simpler. It does not require rocket scientists with multidisciplinary skills and talents working together for decades. However, alignment in the business world requires a keen understanding of customers and what makes them tick plus a large dose of common sense. It can be implemented in a matter of months. Oh and by the way, it does not require $1 billion either! It is, however, the only path to optimal growth.

Before I introduce you to *A4 Precision Alignment*™, I'll share two more examples of mechanical alignment that have influenced how I think about alignment in business.

A puzzling puzzle

Achieving business alignment is a complex puzzle that often eludes even the most experienced management teams. Solving that puzzle is what I have been driven by for more than a decade, since I started to work in management consulting.

I found an elegant metallic puzzle called the Cast Cylinder that was designed by Finnish inventor Vesa Timonen. Timonen is a very creative 3D thinker and tinkerer capable of designing the most perplexing puzzles while using as few pieces as possible.

The challenge is to take Cast Cylinder apart and then reassemble the five pieces. The outside of the cylinder gives absolutely no clues, but inside there is a hidden trick. Like in the business world, a perfect alignment must be achieved to succeed.

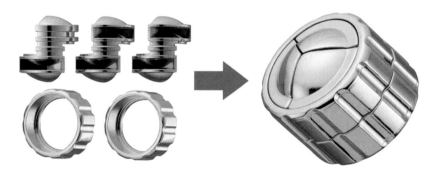

Cast Cylinder puzzle designed by Vesa Timonen

As often happens when solving puzzles, the assembly and disassembly are unsymmetrical. It is actually easier to dismantle the five-piece puzzle than to put it back together. The same applies in business: aligning the various pieces is a lot more challenging than letting the business get misaligned either with its market or internally. It requires careful observations, knowledge and dedication to begin to understand the problems caused by misalignments.

The mechanics of precision alignment

A few years ago, I came across this photo of a Patek Philippe watch, which became the metaphorical representation of my core belief around alignment. What you are looking at here is a piece of precise engineering known as the *29-535 movement.* Unless mistreated, these timepieces will work flawlessly for decades, which is quite remarkable.

Patek Philippe 29-535 movement

This particular movement has a balance wheel that oscillates 28,800 times per hour (frequency of 4 Hz), which means just one single wheel will move over one billion times every four years. This does not include all the other moving gears. You may wonder, as I did, how such a masterpiece continues to work accurately, after billions of movements, year after year. How come we never have to lubricate the mechanisms despite the billions of frictions created by the gears? The answer has two parts: a rigorous design and production as well as a unique use of what is called jewel bearings.

Indulge me here while I get a little timepiece-technical.

In the early days of the mechanical watch, natural jewels such as diamonds, sapphires, rubies and garnets were used. In 1704, two Englishmen, Paul Debaufre and Jacob Debaufre, created a technique to drill hard stones with high precision in order to use them as bearings in mechanical watches.

They received a British patent for their brilliant invention. Two hundred years later, Auguste Verneuil invented a process to make synthetic sapphires and rubies, making jewel bearings much cheaper and more ubiquitous. This process is still used today for all mechanical watches.

Jewel bearings offer many advantages: tiny size and weight, extremely low kinetic and very consistent static friction, pressure and temperature stability, and the ability to work without lubrication, even in acid and corrosive environments. Most importantly, it is their high accuracy and ability to maintain a perfect alignment of gears between the two plates that keep the watches working over decades of use.

Businesses, just as any mechanical watch, need to maintain a perfect alignment with their markets to thrive and grow faster. If gears become misaligned, the watch starts to slow down and eventually stops ticking. If a company loses its market alignment or does not align with new markets, revenues will start to decrease and the company will eventually become irrelevant and die. Misalignments create friction in business transactions and as a consequence, slow down revenue.

John Orcutt, who co-founded Blue Dots with me, and I were fascinated by the beauty and unusual blue color of the jewel bearings in the Patek Philippe 29-535 movement. We chose to use that image and the idea of the blue sapphire jewel bearing alignment as the genesis of our company name: Blue Dots Partners.

As a side note, a mechanical watch needs energy to function, whether from a battery or by manually rewinding the mechanism or automatically drawing kinetic energy from the movement of the wrist during the day. Similarly, a company needs cash (fuel) to function. Some companies need to periodically raise money to get their fuel and some are cash-flow positive, generating their own cash without the need for outside investors.

This begs the question: Is there an equivalent of jewel bearings for a company to maintain its market alignment over time? If so, what are they? How many are they? Do they apply to any type of business? Can alignment be precisely measured? How so?

It turns out those jewel bearings for business exist, in four dimensions that are responsible for a perfect external alignment for any business. **These dimensions or axes are universal, meaning that they exist regardless of what the company does, its size, the type of customers it addresses or what is sold.** This is really the core of what this book is all about. These four dimensions will be described in the chapters ahead, along with internal alignment, the process of aligning all the functions of an organization for successful execution.

Alignment means matching reality and expectations, with components working together in perfect precision relative to one another. It means following a common goal under a common cause. It means having one magnetic north so that all compasses indicate the same direction. It means having the same longitude and latitude system to measure position with a high degree of accuracy and with a common language.

WHAT WE HAVE LEARNED

➤ What do a skydiving world record, docking to the International Space Station, the detection of gravitational waves, a precision watch and a delicate metallic puzzle have in common? This answer is **perfect alignment.**

➤ If only one word could summarize this book, it would be alignment. It is at the core of maximizing growth and generating sustainable shareholder value.

➤ Just as watches rely on jewel bearings to ensure the precise alignment of the gears and plates at the mechanical heart of a timepiece, there are "jewel bearings" for businesses. These universal dimensions exist to establish and maintain a perfect external alignment between a company and its target market.

➤ Internal alignment, the process of aligning all the functions of an organization for flawless execution, is critical for achieving growth.

➤ Our understanding of how these principles work forms the framework for a new, measurable and prescriptive approach to optimizing growth.

NEXT CHAPTER

➤ Introduces the *A4 Precision Alignment*™ methodology to align any business with its target market.

"

When you have alignment, cherish it.

RAY DALIO
Founder, Bridgewater Associates

CHAPTER

3

INTRODUCTION TO THE
A4 PRECISION ALIGNMENT™
PARADIGM

Sylvia's headache

Somewhere in Dedham, Massachusetts, a small town located 22 miles southeast of Boston, a woman named Sylvia Pores is suffering from a persistent headache. She goes to see a pharmacist, who hands her a box of pills to relieve a stomachache. Surprised, the woman says, "My problem is my head, not my stomach."

This encounter illustrates the first axis of alignment: the *Pain* versus the *Claim*. The pharmacist's claim is that his pill will solve a stomachache, not a headache. The woman with her headache pain will definitely not buy the pill.

Now imagine that the pharmacist has the right pill for Sylvia's headache, but there is one problem: he only speaks Korean. Sylvia has never been to Korea and never studied Korean. She can't speak a single word of it. This represents the second axis: *Perception* versus *Message*. Even though it's the right headache pill for Sylvia, costs only 99 cents, and will cure her headache in ten minutes, she will never buy it because she does not understand what the pharmacist is talking about. In other words, the expression of the Claim has not been made clear.

Now imagine the pharmacist speaks perfectly good English and knows about the right pill for Sylvia. He explains to her, "Sure, there is a very effective pill for your headache and it only costs 99 cents, but you have to drive to Boston to get it." Much to Sylvia's dismay, she is not prepared to drive 44 miles back and forth to Boston to get the pill because she is standing in a pharmacy right now with her bad headache! This is the third axis of alignment: *Purchase* versus *Sale*. The manner in which a product or service is delivered in the marketplace has to be aligned with the way customers want to acquire that product or service.

After Sylvia finally gets the headache pill and swallows it, her pain persists and she starts to feel dizzy, with some stomach pain. Clearly, this is not what she expected. She thought her pain would go away in ten minutes and that she would go on with her daily routine. This embodies the fourth and last axis of alignment: *Delight* versus *Offering*, or the gap between the expected experience throughout the entire lifecycle of interactions with the product or service and what is actually delivered by the company.

 Now let's reframe that deceptively simple question I posed in the introduction to this book: What do I do on Monday morning at eight o'clock to realize a perfect alignment?

A new approach to creating sustainable shareholder value

The primary focus of the rest of the book is how to realize external alignment between the company and its target or affinity market. What does alignment mean? What is a pragmatic, realistic and prescriptive way to achieve that complex alignment? Can it be measured? How can it be changed?

I will introduce *A4 Precision Alignment*™, a detailed framework for CEOs, management team members, advisors and board members to put together an action plan in order to know what to do on Monday morning at eight o'clock. This framework provides a fresh new perspective and more importantly, a clear methodology on how to achieve the perfect external market alignment. It's a pragmatic and systematic approach that can be used by any business.

The *A4 Precision Alignment*™ framework is a new way to approach, measure and correct misalignments between any business and its affinity market. It is fundamentally based on what I call the *law of alignment*, i.e. the notion that the optimal growth rate can be achieved only when the company is perfectly aligned with its market.

Any business needs to maximize its alignment to be in the optimal growth state relative to the market it serves. Misalignment increases disruption and friction during the multitude of interactions between the business and its market.

External alignment is based on the four axes, dubbed A1, A2, A3 and A4, and eight dots. The two sides of each of these axes, represented by two dots, have to be perfectly aligned in order to maximize the growth rate of the company.

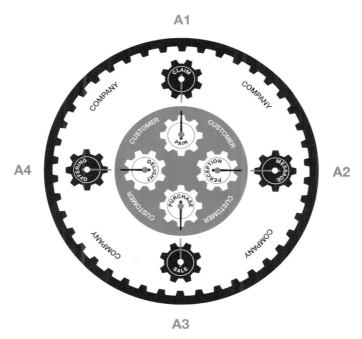

A4 Precision Alignment™ model based on eight dots to align

This concept is all about alignment across four dimensions or along four vectors. In life, we exist in a four-dimensional space. Three of those dimensions are for spatial positioning: two horizontal axes (longitude and latitude) and one vertical (altitude); the fourth dimension is time. To meet someone, you have to be aligned on the four axes, i.e. on the geographic coordinates and at the same time.

Interestingly, in physics, there are four and only four universal forces that govern all interactions between matter and energy: the strong, the weak, the electromagnetic and the gravitational force. That's it. Everything in life and in the universe is happening because of these four forces alone.

The alignments enable you to reach important goals:

ALIGNMENT AXES	CUSTOMER		BUSINESS	GOAL
1	Pain	→ | ←	Claim	Real painkiller
2	Perception	→ | ←	Message	Compelling story
3	Purchase	→ | ←	Sale	Frictionless transaction
4	Delight	→ | ←	Offering	Insane delight

Four axes of alignment

The power of the *A4 Precision Alignment*™ framework is that alignment, or the lack thereof, can be measured precisely along each of the four axes. In Chapter 8, I will describe in detail how these measurements are conducted and how insights are extracted from the data analysis, which then turns into the development of an operating plan, or Growth Playbook as I define it. It is a detailed operating roadmap to realignment that can be executed by the CEO and the management team with discipline, precision and clarity.

This is a new, universal, data-driven, prescriptive methodology to accelerate any business through alignment. This commonsense approach is powerful, and it works because it takes the emotion, gut feelings and subjectivity out of the growth equation. It is a new way to rectify misalignments and optimize growth rates. It enables CEOs and members of the boards of directors to have a common pragmatic and executable plan, always within what I call the *Feasibility Envelope*, which I will cover in Chapter 8.

With the Growth Playbook, CEOs and management teams now know what to do on Monday morning when the clock chimes at eight o'clock.

Traveling through the four axes of alignment

There are four outcome phases when each alignment is realized:

AWARENESS: Once a pain has been recognized and clearly articulated, and the existence of one or several solutions (a claim) has been identified, the first step has been taken toward a possible sales transaction. This is the sine qua non prerequisite to a commerce transaction. It's the *Awareness Phase:* I know I have a problem and I am aware that there is at least one solution to my problem. However, I don't know yet if it's the right solution for me.

FIT: The second axis is focused on what I call the *Fit Phase.* Now that the person who has the pain is aware of the existence of a specific solution to his or her pain, the question becomes: Will that solution be the right one for me? Is there a fit? The understanding on how that particular solution works and solves the problem is critical. The focus is on establishing a match between the expression of the claim and the recognition that it will solve the pain. The outcome of this phase is a buy/no-buy decision; effectively, the Fit Phase serves as the trigger to buy. It is all about being convinced that acquiring the product or service will instantiate the claim and address the pain.

ACQUISITION: The third axis is about acquiring the product or the service. Now that I have decided to buy, how does the transaction take place? How do I take possession of the product or service? How is money exchanged? How will the product or service be delivered to me? This is the *Acquisition Phase.*

CONSUMPTION: The fourth and last axis of alignment is about the experience, based on the full usage lifecycle of the product or service from the very first interaction, the discovery, all the way to the disposal. This is where expected delight and reality meet. This is really the measurement of the satisfaction of the entire usage experience. I call it the *Consumption Phase.* The outcome of this last alignment is the level of customer happiness and the customer's willingness to recommend the product or service to others.

Four phases mapped with the four axes of alignment

Each of the four actions is triggered as a result of alignment. For example, the Pain versus Claim alignment triggers the state of Awareness. The next alignment, Perception versus Message, will trigger the action around Fit, etc.

The last transition, closing the loop from Delight to Awareness, is the word-of-mouth effect. If I am delighted or disappointed with a product or a service, I tell my friends or colleagues, making them aware of the Claim, which they will match or not with their own Pain. This is all about the consumer propensity to evangelize (positively or negatively) to others and be an ambassador or detractor for a product or service. This action plays a large role in contributing to the growth or lack thereof of the business. This is how the notion of Net Promoter Score (NPS) was born, which is a score based on a simple question:

66 How likely is it that you would recommend our company/product/service to a friend or colleague?

Each step presents an opportunity for the person who is going through that step to share positive or negative feedback, contributing to business growth or decline. This is the catalyst and where the hidden, undiscovered but critical and mighty forces of growth come into play. It's make-or-break for the company, its employees and shareholders. This is what truly matters.

In more detail, here is how the dynamic of the four alignments works:

AXES OF ALIGNMENT	PHASES	OUTPUT OF A SUCCESSFUL ALIGNMENT
A1	Awareness	I am fully aware of my pain and that there are solutions to address it out there.
A2	Fit	I understand there is a match between the claim and what I am looking for to solve my pain and made the decision to buy.
A3	Acquisition	I have gone through the process of acquiring the product or the service but have not used it yet.
A4	Delight	I have used the product or service and if what I expected is what I received, then I am delighted and I can spread the word.

Results for next step after each alignment

Another way to think about this dynamic is that there are only three reasons prospects don't buy:

- They don't feel the pain.

- They don't understand how your company will alleviate their pain.

- They want to buy, but the modality of acquisition is not what they expect.

There are only two reasons customers stop using your product:

- Their pain is gone without your offering.

- They are not happy with the product or service anymore (for example, because pricing became too high) and someone else has a claim that is significantly better (i.e. worth the trouble of switching).

Alignment of the pain and the claim triggers the curiosity to explore and determine if there is a fit. If there is a fit and the second alignment is realized, as a result, the decision to buy is made. The third alignment is all about the execution of the transaction. Finally, the fourth alignment is about consuming the product and ideally experiencing the expected delight.

The four axes of alignment at work

Pain versus Claim → Awareness

Over the years, I have acquired 240 CDs that have been sitting in a closet in my living room. They have accumulated a decent layer of dust that I periodically combat (I seem to always lose in the end). My CD collection became a joyful playground for spiders and all kinds of other six-legged insects, which my daughter abhors. I can't even remember the last time I opened a jewel case and popped a CD in my player. Before 2017 ended, I put on my list of New Year's resolutions to dispose of all my CDs in 2018. My plan was to give them to the local library and hopefully give someone the opportunity to enjoy my exotic musical tastes, extending from Daniel Balavoine to Henri Vieuxtemps' Concerto No. 5 in A minor. My goal was to get rid of all my CDs, while maintaining the ability to listen to my favorite music in the comfort of my living room or from 35,000 feet above the ground on a flight to Hawaii. Making digital copies of all those CDs sounded far too painful.

I was already aware of some streaming music services such as Apple Music, Amazon Music Unlimited, Pandora, Slacker and of course Spotify.

Perception versus Message → Fit

After doing some research and asking for advice, particularly from my daughter who is an avid music listener, I started to research Spotify. I tested it and realized that it had the vast majority of the songs held in my dusty CD collection. I concluded that this would be a good solution to my problem and decided to go for it.

Purchase versus Sale → Acquisition

I tried the free version for a few days and no surprise, did not like the advertising and the fact that I could not store my own playlists. However, I decided to take advantage of their free 30-day trial and then pay $9.99 per month. It was an easy experience and it worked flawlessly.

Delight versus Offering → Consumption Experience

The discovery phase of the experience was great. It was simple to set up on my iPhone and on our new Amazon Echo. I really enjoyed the ability to start listening to a piece on one device and seamlessly continue on another. Building playlists of my favorite music was easy, and I enjoyed discovering the Daily Mix that was proposed and cleverly built based on my musical tastes. I could also download music in advance before boarding a plane for a long flight to visit a client in New York. I quickly became a big fan.

It's no wonder that as of March 31, 2018, Spotify had more than 75 million paid subscribers to its music service and over 170 million active users. It went public in April 2018 and as of July 31, 2018, was worth close to $33 billion.

The hidden power of the *A4 Precision Alignment*™ paradigm

In math, there is an elegant and effective way to solve certain differential equations. It is called the separation of variables (also known as the Fourier method invented by Joseph Fourier, a French mathematician and physicist born in 1768). When possible, it allows the equation to be written in such a way that each variable appears on one side so that it can be very eloquently solved.

The same principle applies to the *A4 Precision Alignment*™ paradigm. It is what I call the *Separation of Alignments*. How does it work? The important notion here is that each of the four axes acts independently from the others. The same way variables are separated in the Fourier method, the four axes of alignment are treated independently. Now, of course, they are all related to the fundamental premise of the business and its market, the same ways variables are related to the same equation. This notion of relative independence is profound because now, a company can focus on addressing a misalignment along one of the four axes and does not have to worry about creating other problems or additional misalignments along the three other axes. **Effectively, each axis acts independently, and it's the alignment of all four axes that creates the perfect alignment that will produce the optimal growth rate for the business.**

The universality of alignment

The power of the *A4 Precision Alignment*™ framework is that it is universal; it applies to every business. From Ford to Ferrari, from Wells Fargo to Bank of Hawaii, from United Airlines to KLM, it doesn't matter what the company does. It does not matter how big or small the company is, as long as it is generating some revenue. It applies to businesses selling to consumers (B2C) or businesses selling to businesses (B2B) or to government (B2G). In the end, any business, no matters what it does, where it is located, how it sells or how small or big, must address a well-identified pain, must articulate its claim in a way that it is well understood, must provide an easy way to sell and must delight its customers. This is why this alignment approach is truly universal.

There is, however, one caveat to this new approach: the measurement of alignment, as Chapter 8 will cover, can be done only if the company is big enough. So what is big enough? What matters is the number of customers, more so than the level of revenue. To measure alignment, I estimate the required number of customers is about 50 at a minimum. If the company is too small, it simply does not have enough data for an analysis to be statistically correct and for true insights to be extracted. In fact, it may be misleading to draw any conclusions based on a handful of current customers or lost customers. However, even with a low number of customers, the company won't be successful or maintain its growth rate if it loses alignment across one or more axes.

There are two points to adjust to realize alignment

In each of the four axes of alignment there are two points to align. Alignment, or misalignment, can happen by changing just one of these two points. Companies tend to want to change what they do or how they do it because they feel they have more control, but interestingly enough, the best options for achieving alignment lie outside the company and get overlooked. They miss the opportunity to change the prospect or customer segments and improve alignment without changing what they do. It is also possible to change the behavior of customers by changing perceptions, behaviors and habits. This has been well documented in the work of the authors of *Influencer: The Power to Change Anything* or *Hooked* by Nir Eyal or *The Power of Habit* by Charles Duhigg.

This reminds me of an old joke. It goes like this. Two men were driving in a truck. The truck got stuck in a tunnel because the clearance of the tunnel was not high enough compared to the height of the truck. The driver had an idea. He looked at the tires and started to let some air out to deflate them so that the top of the truck would no longer scrape the ceiling of the tunnel. His colleague jumped out of the truck and yelled at him, "You are crazy! Why are you doing this to the tires? It's the top of the truck that is scraping the ceiling, not the bottom!"

Here is an example of what I mean by looking at both points of alignment. In our first axis, A1, the pain and the claim must be aligned. Many companies tend to focus on the claim, because it is based on what they design, build and master. However, sometimes there is a better way: looking at the other side of the equation, or the pain. Doing precision segmentation can uncover prospects for whom the Pain is actually far more acute and exacerbated by other factors that may have been overlooked. For example, if a company has developed a small device that people carry on their wrist to alert their doctor in case they don't feel well, instead of marketing the device to elderly people at risk of falling or fainting at home, epileptic adults might be a better market.

Another example of what I call "moving the other point" is changing the expectation. It would be futile for McDonald's to make people think that their burgers are as good as Argentine beef from free-ranging cows around the pampas. Instead of changing the claim, McDonald's can simply focus on the pain and go after people who want to eat quickly for no more than a couple of bucks.

The magic of expectation

Many years ago, Peter Wolken, one of the fathers of venture capital, who created Associated Ventures Investors (AVI) back in 1982 and was one of my VC mentors, told me about the millionaires' magician. Wolken attended one of his famous parlor magic shows in New York. I had never heard of the millionaires' magician. His name is Steve Cohen and for many years, he performed his famous show to the delight of small audiences at the Waldorf Astoria hotel.

Cohen is really in the business of delivering wonder. Why does it work? It is simply because he beats expectations, and by a large margin. When he performs, the outcome is never anticipated. The tricks are unsettling and contrary to the laws of physics that govern our world. But not in Cohen's world. He is driven by triggering a twinkle of light in the eyes of his audience through the unexpected.

In his signature trick, Think-A-Drink, he asks one member of the audience to think of a drink, any drink. He works his magic on a teapot and serves a drink in a glass and ta-da, the liquid served is exactly the drink the person suggested. Most of us would never expect that magically, the exact drink imagined would appear in a teapot. The magic exists because our expectation was beaten by a large factor.

A mismatch between expectations and reality can have some serious negative consequences. It happens to all of us: we walk down a flight of stairs and we miss the last step. Why? Because in our brain, there is an image that does not include that last step. So when our brain commands our body to initiate the right movement to negotiate the landing, we lose our balance and dignity when we fall in front of a dismayed audience.

Expectation management is important to realize alignment. It is critical for a company to control it across the four axes of alignment and to regularly assess whether these expectations, formed in the brains of prospects and customers, are what the company indeed will deliver. Like product management, expectations should be constantly managed and refined. They are the ultimate reason alignments are realized or missed.

The next four chapters are double-clicking on each of the four axes of alignment with some specific examples on how the alignment framework can be implemented.

How companies lose alignment

There are two scenarios under which companies lose their alignment: unforced and forced.

Internal decisions can create misalignment along any of the four axes. I call this unforced misalignment. It might be as a result of poor decisions the company made along the way, such as a lack of focus or losing sight of what matters most for the customer. It could also be because the company extended its business into adjacent products or services and missed the fact that the same customers they have been successfully serving might not have the same pain level for the new product as for their core product.

Here are some examples of unforced misalignment for each of the four axes:

- **A1 PAIN VERSUS CLAIM MISALIGNMENT** In 1999, Cosmopolitan, a magazine focused on well-being and sex tips for young women, decided to launch a Greek yogurt cleverly called Cosmopolitan Yogurt. The idea was based on survey data indicating that 65% of their readers consumed food in their bedrooms. Needless to say, the yogurt was a total flop. It left customers baffled, and the price of the "special" yogurt was significantly higher than other similar products. Within 18 months, the brand was discontinued. This reminds me of Colgate getting in the frozen food business with its Colgate Kitchen Entrees brand of lasagna and Swedish meatballs. These are good examples of a total A1 misalignment: the company imagined a pain that their customers did not really have and offered a less attractive Claim compared to other established companies.

- **A2 PERCEPTION VERSUS MESSAGE MISALIGNMENT** In May 2002, PricewaterhouseCoopers (doing business as PwC) decided to spin out its technology consulting business and gave it the name Monday. Not only is Monday the least popular day of the week, the initiative was confusing and did not carry the professionalism, differentiation and trust of the PwC brand. According to Gartner, PwC had planned to invest $110 million to establish the new brand. The name was profusely ridiculed and was abandoned a year later. This example will remain in the annals as a wild A2 misalignment.

- **A3 PURCHASE VERSUS SALE MISALIGNMENT** In July 2006, Dell launched into the retail business with over 100 mall kiosks called Dell Direct Stores. It also launched two 3,000-square-foot mall stores: one in Dallas and the other in New York. Dell wanted to emulate Apple, but there was a catch: you could not buy a computer there! The stores were designed for customers to test-drive equipment and then place an online order. In January 2008, the company announced the closure of its 140 U.S. kiosk outlets and its intent to focus on what Dell does best: selling over the phone and online. The notion of a customer going into a computer retail store without being able to buy is a prime example of an A3 grossly missed alignment (although some joke that today, Best Buy is the showcase for Amazon!).

- **A4 EXPECTATION VERSUS OFFERING MISALIGNMENT**
  In April 1985, the Coca-Cola Company introduced a
  new formulation for the iconic brand called New Coke[5].
  Consumers expected to enjoy the drink as much as, if not
  more than, the original Coke. They did not like it and 79
  days after its introduction, Coca-Cola returned to its original
  product and rebranded it Coca-Cola Classic, resulting in a
  significant uptick in sales.

Loss of alignment can also be triggered by external forces. I call this forced misalignment. This is when innovation disrupts the status quo and can become the engine of the insane growth described in Chapter 1. Innovation can materialize along any of the four axes.

Here is a way to best think about how disruptive innovation can affect alignment. Imagine a customer is like a compass. If a new and strong-enough magnetic field is introduced, the compass needle rotates to align itself with the new magnetic field and "forgets" the old, weaker field. When a new company successfully innovates along one of the four axes, it is effectively creating a different and powerful magnetic field. Customers, like a compass, want to align themselves along that new magnetic field. These new companies, called category creators, upend the level playing field and challenge the status quo. Here are some examples:

- **A1 DISRUPTION** Airbnb turned the hospitality industry on its head by offering a cozier, less expensive lodging experience, challenging many claims made by hotels.

- **A2 DISRUPTION** Nike changed the perception of athletic shoes with its iconic Just Do It slogan created 30 years ago. Very early on, Nike understood the importance of selecting the right customer target and demographic, as well as the power of instilling a sense of emotion and desire for community into the brand. Many (myself included) believe the Nike slogan was so effective because it articulated the prevailing attitude of the highly independent and overly skeptical Gen X market.

- **A3 DISRUPTION** Amazon disrupted the book retailing industry by introducing an easy way for people to discover

---

5   The infamous New Coke debacle became a legendary marketing case. Malcolm Gladwell goes into great depth in his book *Blink*.

and buy books through a strong customer-centric experience. Amazon forced traditional bookstores to evolve and offer new experiences.

- **A4 DISRUPTION** Uber offered a much better car transportation experience than the old taxi industry that has not changed for decades.

One final thought: A startup that is trying to build a large business, say over $100 million in sales, has to make a prediction on where the market will be in the future. The most innovative startups that win are the ones that define and will control a new and powerful magnetic field in a few years. In their formative years, they have to possess a strong point of view that articulates their vision and why it is different and truly transformative. In fact, it will be so powerful that it will seriously mute the competition. This is the idea that Peter Thiel articulates so well in his *Zero to One* book about building, protecting and maintaining monopolies.

APPLE

A perfect alignment along each axis

Let's look at Apple and understand why it became the poster child of perfect alignment.

Many ideas, points of view and opinions have been shared on why Apple has become such a successful company and the first to be worth more than $1 trillion. Some argue it was Steve Jobs's genius; some consider it the user experience. Others claim that it's the symbiotic combination of the hardware and the software, or the emotional, product-centric and well-crafted advertising campaigns. While all are reasonable arguments, the real answer is because Apple, like very few other companies, has realized a perfect alignment across the four axes.

➤ **A1 ALIGNMENT:** The pain Apple addresses is not only the coolness factor but the abjection most consumers have for technology. People don't want to deal with things that don't work right away and aren't seamlessly intuitive. They don't want to research how to fix a technical problem. People do want to possess a beautiful object they are proud to own and love to share and exhibit, as long as it works magically. The real claim that Apple offers is empathy. Apple understands this better than any other technology company and at a very deep level. It is ingrained in its DNA. The idea that a customer would suffer by using an Apple product was inconceivable to Jobs. Apple's products simply work and because of their beautiful design, make owners proud. In the end, they have to work, almost flawlessly. Can you imagine a beautiful Bentley that has problems with its engine, windows or heater? Coolness in itself is not enough. It has to work beautifully. Apple's products impute desirability.

➤ **A2 ALIGNMENT:** The message Apple has diligently crafted over the years is remarkable. It started with the legendary 1984 Super Bowl ad that introduced the Macintosh. This ad has endured over decades as a powerful contrast between a young, aggressive, thinking-outside-the-box company and the old, unimaginative and unexciting establishment exemplified by IBM. Apple never wanted to be better. It always wanted to be different, hence the 1997 Think Different ad campaign that celebrates the "crazy ones, the misfits, the rebels, the trouble-makers." Apple challenges the status quo through its creative passion for changing people's lives and pushing the envelope. The iPod ad showing silhouettes of people dancing to the beat of their creative self is another example of strong identification and sense of belonging. Apple users want to identify and be part of Apple's manifesto of changing the world.

➤ **A3 ALIGNMENT:** Apple understands that the customer journey starts way before the user actually touches the product. It starts with the message and continues with the way people acquire its product. When I worked at Apple, I proposed the idea that the company should sell direct on the internet, then founded and ran the Worldwide Internet Commerce group at Apple. I understood, back in 1996, that we needed to let consumers configure and buy a Mac on the internet. For the first time in Apple's history, we wanted to establish a direct, emotional connection with our customers. We delivered an online store that won many awards and still represents billions in revenue for Apple today. Later, Apple completely redefined the retail experience, incorporating many innovative ideas in a physical retail location. This is why Apple's stores are the most profitable in the world. According to research companies eMarketer and CoStar, in 2017, Apple stores generated $5,546 per square foot. By comparison, Tiffany & Co has sales of $2,951 per square foot, top gasoline retailer Murphy USA comes in at $3,721 per square foot and Lululemon Athletica, the leading apparel retailer, at $1,560 per square foot.

➤ **A4 ALIGNMENT:** The perfect alignment on the fourth axis is about delivering delight, and Apple has no doubt raised that bar higher than any other company in the world. From the discovery phase, where the user touches and opens the box for the very first time, all the way to the disposal phase of bringing an old Apple product to the store for it to be recycled, Apple has masterfully crafted every single step of that delightful journey. It is not by accident that the packaging of any Apple product is so beautiful. It triggers emotions. It invites discovery. It gives pleasure. Apple's technical support is unparalleled. Apple Genius Bar employees will do whatever it takes to fix your Mac, no matter how long it takes or how hard the problem. They will not hesitate to replace the product if need be. They are known for their patience and great attitudes. You feel safe, respected and heard with them, never disparaged or challenged.

CASE STUDY

WHAT WE HAVE LEARNED

➤ There are four and only four axes of external alignment:

1. Pain ⟷ Claim
2. Perception ⟷ Message
3. Purchase ⟷ Sale
4. Delight ⟷ Offering

➤ The *A4 Precision Alignment*™ methodology is truly universal and works for any business regardless of its size, type, industry, geographic location or business model. It can be applied to a café in Paris or Walmart.

➤ Each alignment is independent in the sense that it can be measured (assuming the company has more than 50 customers) and addressed without the risk of creating misalignment along any of the other axes.

➤ Misalignment on any of these four dimensions will cause revenue to slow down.

➤ The four axes of alignment map perfectly and sequentially with the customer journey: Awareness → Fit → Acquisition → Consumption.

➤ Alignment can be lost through two different mechanisms:

• Unforced: Companies not paying attention to their customers (degrading experience) or going after adjacent paths of growth that are not as relevant to their core customers.

• Forced: A new "magnetic field" created by innovative companies introducing a new user experience with a strong and real differentiation.

CASE STUDY

➤ Apple: a perfect alignment along each axis

NEXT CHAPTER

➤ Focuses on A1, the first axis of alignment: Pain versus Claim.

"

We often found ourselves in the position
of explaining the problem, not the solution,
to our customers.

BILL BONNER
author

FIRST AXIS

Pain versus Claim

ALIGNMENT AXES	CUSTOMER		BUSINESS	GOAL
1	Pain	→ | ←	Claim	Real painkiller
2	Perception	→ | ←	Message	Compelling story
3	Purchase	→ | ←	Sale	Frictionless transaction
4	Delight	→ | ←	Offering	Insane delight

The first sales transaction is the true beginning of any new business. After months of product development and preparation, excitement sets in. It all starts with receiving the very first dollar from the very first customer. That very first dollar would never be captured without the Pain and the Claim being aligned. Both have to be in resonance.

So, the first question is: What constitutes pain? Is this pain or a desire? What's the difference?

Until the automobile was invented in 1886, nobody felt the pain of not having one, precisely because it did not exist. In a way, the pain became instantiated or expressed only once the automobile was invented and a legitimate claim was articulated. Of course, the pain of walking five miles to buy something or riding in a carriage for days and days to visit distant family members was there, but it remained unaddressed because no other solution existed. People lived with the current way of transport. It was both accepted and expected. Today, it's the same: we are not feeling the pain of not being able to travel from San Francisco to Paris in one hour at an average speed of 5,600 miles per hour, because we know there is no way to do it. No legitimate and credible claim exists to accomplish that feat. But most probably, 50 years from now it will be natural to do it and future generations will say: How was it possible that in 2020, people spent 10 hours sitting on a vintage, noisy and polluting Airbus A380?

In April 2017, a gadget started to spread in schools across the world: the fidget spinner. Scott McCoskery invented it in 2014. The device was initially called the Torqbar. What pain did it address? Being bored in class? Wanting a way to show off and brag? Wanting a new approach to make friends and share something new? Wanting to get the attention of the teacher? Or simply wanting to be cool? Before the fidget spinner was invented, that particular pain did not exist or perhaps was addressed in other ways. Once the gadget started to appear, the pain of not having one became real.

As a venture capitalist, I have heard the same question so many times: **"Is it a painkiller or a vitamin?"** In my mind, both can work and result in real businesses. The critical question is: how big is this market? Very successful companies have built large businesses on vitamins not painkillers, figuratively or not. For example, Vitacost, a company based in Boca Raton, Florida, is such a company, selling dietary supplements.

When I stood in line on December 15, 2017 to see *Star Wars: The Last Jedi* and pay $14.50 to watch the saga for 152 minutes, what was my pain? It was the desire to be entertained for two hours that prompted me to spend the money and enjoy the company of a friend I had not seen for three months. According to the Motion Pictures Association of

America, the worldwide box office market reached $38.6 billion in 2016. Audiences between the ages of 18 and 24 attended an average of seven movies during the year. In the US and Canada alone, there were 1.32 billion tickets sold that year, grossing $11.4 billion. No one would mind owning a piece of that "vitamin" industry.

Pain and Claim always works in tandem, like day and night. Once cannot exist without the other. In other words, with no credible claim, there is no expressed pain and therefore no market. In other words, there cannot be an exchange of money for a solution to alleviate the pain. The paradox is that the pain might exist, but it is in a latent stage until a real solution is found.

The "Pain of Negation"

A few years ago, I was asked by a CEO, "If I go see the 49ers play against the Bears, what pain is being addressed?" I pondered his thoughtful question. One did not decide to see a game because of a sudden pain that needed to be appeased.

So, what is it?

Indeed, there is a pain and in a way, it's a hidden pain. I call it the *Pain of Negation*. The pain is created by the notion of missing out, not getting the dopamine in the brain. It is also known as Fear of Missing Out, or FOMO.

Of course, in the example of watching a movie, the claim is that I will be entertained for two hours and 32 minutes, not counting the movie previews and getting comfortable in a nice seat. The calculation is that I am willing to pay $14.50 for that entertainment, enjoyment that would be missed if I did not go to the theater. It certainly beats a skydive that costs $260 for a tandem jump from 13,000 feet, i.e. about $5.20 per second compared to two-tenths of a penny per second to enjoy the latest Bond.

The Pain of Negation generally applies to pleasure created by all sorts of activities. It is the notion of not getting what one craves. It is real and it is painful. The claim on the other side alleviates it by delivering the expected pleasure or satisfaction at an acceptable price point.

How big is the pain of missing out? It really depends. In the case of a movie, it is fairly mild. If you are intent on spending a week in Maui and for whatever reason you can't, then the pain is much higher. In some cases, it can be tremendously high (no pun intended) and life-threatening, like in drug addiction.

Where does price fit in the *A4 Precision Alignment*™ methodology?

Price is one of the most important components of the claim. In fact, no claim should be made without pricing. This is akin to a medicine prescription without the dosage, i.e. the frequency and amount of medicine that is appropriate to take. The claim concerns the medical condition the medicine addresses, secondary effects that have been observed and how some restrictions may apply. The dosage is equivalent to the cost of a product. No one would take a medicine without knowing how many pills are needed, what the dosage is and how often to take it. Similarly, no one would make the decision to buy a product or a service without knowing its cost.

Imagine you want to buy a new car, a ticket to see a U2 concert or a bottle of red Bordeaux, yet no one can tell you the price. Would you buy? Of course not! In fact, the question itself does not make real sense. How can you buy something without knowing the price? Price/cost is a necessary but not sufficient component of the A1 alignment. Also, terms of payments have to be part of the claim. Most people in the US could not afford to buy a $300,000 home if they had to pay the entire amount up front. What makes the transaction possible is the ability to finance the home with a bank-issued mortgage.

Here's a complex question that product manufacturers and service providers have to address: What is the optimal pricing?

Optimizing pricing can be formulated in a simple equation. In fact, what needs to be optimized is not pricing, but the following:

(Price - Cost) × (Volume Sold – Volume Returned)

Cost includes variables such as cost of goods, cost of sales and cost of support. If the price is too low, then while the volume sold can be high, the cost might be higher than the price. The business can never be profitable, as it would lose money on every order. The unit economics don't work. While this can be a market development strategy (loss leader), it is not sustainable over a period of time. Startups take this approach all the time, with the capital needed to cover product costs funded by VCs or PE firms. This is the "land grab" scenario, one of the hallmarks of Silicon Valley. It's the reason Uber, Airbnb and Lyft can exist. Eventually, the question of profitability and self-funding has to be resolved. In a more mature business, it can work if the revenue generated by other products can cover the loss (both by negative gross margin and amortization of fixed costs) incurred by the loss leader products.

If the price is too high compared to expectation, the volume sold might be too low and revenue generated won't be sufficient to cover all operating and fixed costs. Profitability will be a struggle in that scenario.

In some cases, the price might be low enough, but volume cannot be delivered. For example, this can occur when a new hot product comes out and manufacturing cannot meet demand. This is what happened when the Tesla Model 3 was released. Or consider the good restaurant that serves exquisite food at a reasonable price but does not have enough tables to seat all patrons. While scarcity can create buzz and drive further demand, ultimately frustration will hurt the business. Another factor in optimizing the price equation is to understand and anticipate churn triggered by the price increase.

I do not believe in giving things away. Growing a real business from free products is very difficult, unless it is the teaser that is free[6]. There is simply no business without an exchange of money for goods or services. For example, getting a purchase order in the software security

---

6   However, enhanced value by offering something additional for free can be one of the more cost-effective ways of getting a better price for the core product. In behavioral economics, free can be worth a lot.

business is very hard, especially if the product has been given for free or the market has been educated and trained to not pay. It's the kiss of death to growth. I have seen this scenario too many times with start-ups doing a proof of concept for free and then being surprised when the customer does not want to buy their $350,000 product. The customer was just doing testing, most likely to learn something. Similarly, price promotions are very risky. Like painkillers, they should be used sparingly and only when absolutely needed.

APERTURE INVESTORS

A good pricing alignment

In October 2018, Peter Kraus launched Aperture Investors, a $4 billion firm dedicated to active asset management. Kraus is a veteran of the asset management industry, with four decades of experience. He is recognized for having turned around AllianceBernstein as chairman and CEO after the 2008 financial meltdown. Previously, Kraus worked at Merrill Lynch and Goldman Sachs as co-head of Investment Management. Kraus started Aperture with a radically different approach to the fees it charges clients. He defined the firm as "active management with accountability." The difference with Kraus' approach is that fees are based on performance. If the firm does not beat some previously identified passive ETFs (exchange-traded funds), then the client is charged the same fee as charged by these stated benchmark ETF funds, to cover their lower-than-industry salary and overhead. Kraus' idea came from the observation that there were way too many managers managing passive and index-trading funds whose compensation was not aligned with the interest of their clients. Presumably, the idea is that funds managed by savvy human beings should outperform those that are passively managed by computer algorithms. This justifies the payment of higher fees to uncover alphas (i.e. excess returns compared to the market). The problem is that the majority of funds did not even beat the market. Interestingly, Kraus also designed the compensation structure so that the manager would not take inconsiderable risk, because the compensation is reset every year and a large portion of the compensation is actually put back into the fund, and you have to earn the client the return that generated the initial compensation.

Another similar example is what Eric Benhamou, the former CEO of networking company 3Com, did when he started the Palo Alto-based VC firm Benhamou Global Ventures. The firm does not charge management fees to its limited partners. However, they distribute the carried interest on a deal-by-deal basis with no clawback. Performance and compensation are now aligned. LPs (limited partners) and GPs (general partners) are aligned.

CASE STUDY

Other critical variables besides price

There are other variables that play an essential role in A1 alignment.

Here is an example to illustrate this concept. Let's assume that next month I have an important dinner meeting in Washington, DC and I need to fly there from Sacramento, California. I search Expedia for all the flights on the day I want to leave and review other things like: Which airlines? How many stops? Is there no direct flight? Can I use my mileage program? What are the times of departure and arrival? Do they have aisle seats toward the front of the cabin? Do I have to pay for my luggage? Is there a meal served onboard? What about entertainment? And of course, how much does the ticket cost?

In this equation, price is one of the many variables. In some cases, it may be the most important one (such as for a student with little money). In other cases, price may not be much of a consideration. For example, if I have a dinner meeting in Washington, the time I land must be taken into account, as well as the time it will take me to go to my hotel, get ready and ride to the restaurant. I am willing to pay a reasonable premium to make sure that the time will work out for my important meeting.

Now, I know there are other solutions to my problem: I could charter a private jet. The round trip would cost about $120,000 on a heavy jet. A Falcon 900 or Gulfstream IV costs about $7,000 to $9,000 per hour. It would be a lot more comfortable, convenient (no stop, and I can leave at whatever time I want) and the service on board would certainly be unparalleled. Now, the reality is that this claim is not aligned at all with my pain. There is no match. It's not even close. The price is way above what I can pay. But just because I cannot pay does not mean there is no business for companies like NetJets. They simply target a different market segment of executive or wealthy individuals who are willing to pay a lot for convenience and comfort.

There are other cases where price is not the problem. I may have decided to buy a car at a certain price, but the manufacturer does not have the exact features I need, so I won't buy it. Sometimes, payment terms are more important than price itself. I may be willing to buy the car I would not have bought otherwise, because they offered 0% interest on a 60-month loan.

So, to trigger a purchasing decision, there is a defined set of variables that matter greatly to the person making the decision. I call them *Contextual Variables* because they matter to the specific person having the pain and are very specific to that person's situation. **It is important for whoever is making the claim to understand these Contextual Variables, so that alignment can be realized.**

Preaching the gospel of the claim

As explained at the beginning of the chapter, the existence of a legitimate claim materializes the pain. In other words, the problem may have been latent before, because no one thought it could be solved in a real, pragmatic and economical way. **The speed at which the awareness of a legitimate claim spreads is a key factor in how fast a market grows, which affects the top-line growth rate of all participants in that market.**

At the peak, demand is very high, driving low inventory and scarcity, which creates pricing hikes. If the awareness is too low, the company is ahead of the market. When awareness is at the peak, it is too late for a new player to enter the market as incumbents have already commanded most of the market share. When a company evolves in a very dynamic market, i.e. a market with a high growth rate, it is much harder to gain market share. This is why being the early player that initially dominates the market gives that company a true and unfair competitive advantage.

It is when the pain and claim reach a certain equilibrium that the market becomes mature. This is the case for the automotive industry. At that point, the market dynamic is very different: it is all about stealing market share from other players. When there are several products on the market, fairly undifferentiated, all competing for the same dollar, trying to convince a customer to switch from one to another is a tall order and an expensive endeavor. In other words, the cost of customer acquisition is increasing as we travel through the claim awareness curve, as the graph on the next page shows:

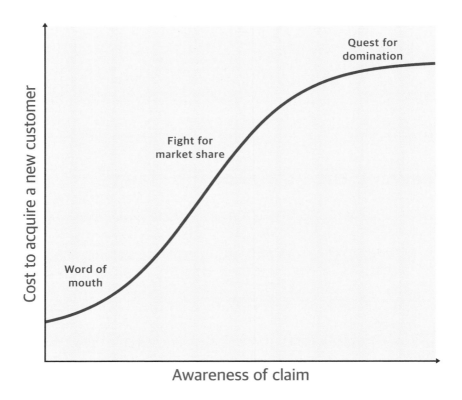

Cost of customer acquisition as a function of claim awareness

So, when figuring out a growth strategy, understanding where we are on the claim awareness curve is critical, as it will dictate the type of growth strategy to choose and the required capital and talent to execute it.

The awareness of a claim spreads like a wave, and the velocity at which the awareness spreads dictates the adoption rate of the product. Typically, the spread of awareness of a claim follows a Gaussian curve:

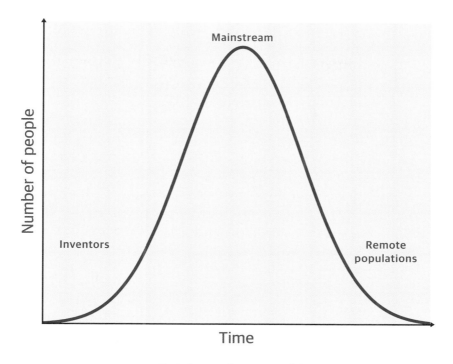

Typical curve of awareness of claim

At the beginning, the inventors who identify the claim are the only ones who know about it. As the claim spreads, the number of people who become aware of it grows, and the claim becomes so popular that the curve reaches a peak. This is the point when most people have heard about it. Finally, the claim reaches more remote populations.

The speed at which a claim spreads throughout the world is a function of two factors:

1. The magnitude of the problem it solves
2. The speed at which information circulates (network effect)

If a research team, anywhere in the world, were able to find a cure for lung and bronchial cancer, the deadliest cancer of all, the news of that discovery would spread around the globe in a matter of minutes or hours. This is due to both the importance and the magnitude of the claim (i.e. its impact on a large portion of the population) and the existence of the internet and social networks, which amplify and greatly accelerate the circulation of news.

LEVI STRAUSS & CO

A solid A1 alignment

On January 24, 1848, James W. Marshall found gold at Sutter's Mill, just outside Sacramento, California. From that day on until 1855, is it estimated that 300,000 people traveled to California to participate in the Gold Rush. Many businesses flourished during that period providing equipment, food, lodging, entertainment, tools and health care to support the 49ers. It was during that first year of extraordinary movement that Levi Strauss left Bavaria in Germany and arrived in New York to work with his half-brothers in their dry-goods business, named J. Strauss Brother & Company. Looking to make his fortune, Strauss moved to San Francisco in 1953. He named his business Levi Strauss, which operated as a branch of his half-brothers' company. Most of the goods sold were for miners, but then families started to purchase clothing for women and children.

In 1872, a tailor from Reno named Jacob Davis who frequently purchased denim from Strauss came up with an idea. He observed that his customers' pants were wearing too fast and wanted to design much stronger clothing. His idea was to use rivets to reinforce the areas where pants were wearing out too quickly. Davis partnered with Strauss and a patent was granted for the genius invention in May 1873. The first pair of Levi's 501 jeans was sold in the 1890s.

Blue jeans evolved from a blue-collar staple to a cultural phenomenon in the 1950s. The Levi's brand flourished, its popularity exemplified by many icons wearing the iconic pants, including John Wayne, Marlon Brando and Albert Einstein.

The company has experienced tremendous success. Revenue peaked in 1997 at $7.1 billion, although the company's revenue declined to $4 billion in 2000 as a result of stronger competition from retailers such as Walmart and Gap. In 2011, Chip Bergh became president and CEO and in 2016, Levi's bought the naming rights for the NFL's San Francisco 49ers' new stadium in Santa Clara for $220 million, to be paid over 20 years. Revenues reached $4.6 billion in 2016 and climbed to $5.8 billion by year-end 2018, with income of $283 million. The company went public on March 21, 2019, at a price of $17 per share. At the end of that month,

CASE STUDY

the stock was trading at $22.41, giving the company a market cap of $8.9 billion. At the time of the IPO, the company operated about 2,900 retail stores, and its products continue to be sold in about 50,000 retail locations across 110 countries.

By understanding the need for sturdier pants, Strauss and Davis were able to build an amazing business that continues to thrive almost 150 years later. A1 alignment has played a key role in the company's success.

SEGWAY

A dramatic A1 misalignment

On December 3, 2001, on the ABC *Good Morning America* program, a company called Segway introduced a two-wheeled self-balancing "human transporter." It became one of the most hyped products ever launched, touted as revolutionizing the transportation industry forever. Pundits predicted it would be larger than the internet. Steve Jobs said that Segway was "as big a deal as the PC." It was supposed to solve the last-mile problem in cities and dense urban areas across the world. Dean Kamen, its genius inventor and well-respected engineering leader, had created a marvel of engineering, with its two brushless DC electric motors, its gyroscopes for balancing and computer-driven drive-by-wire technology.

Sales began in early 2002. By 2007, Segway had only reached a mere 1% of its projected sales. It was a commercial disaster. Segway is now relegated to cops and tourists. Its flagship product became a punch line.

What happened?

Its commercial failure can be explained by a misalignment along the A1 axis on several fronts:

- **PERCEPTION.** Right from the get-go, it suffered from a strong negative "dork factor." It was never socially accepted. People riding Segways were considered nerds buying ridiculous toys.

- **PRICE.** Its price tag of $4,950 was way too high, probably about five times more than what consumers were willing to pay for the product. Indeed, a much more reasonable price would have been around $1,000, which happens to be what Apple charged for an iPhone X.

- **SAFETY.** People expected the Segway to be safe, and it was for the most part. However, the tragic death in September 2010 of millionaire Jimi Heselden, the owner of the company, after plunging off a cliff while riding his Segway, along with the well-publicized fall of President George W. Bush in 2003 and numerous other accidents, did not help. Most cities had ordinances requiring riders to wear a helmet to avoid serious injuries or death.

- **CONVENIENCE.** Users expected to ride it on sidewalks, but some cities and municipalities did not allow that, forcing drivers to use it on the streets. Parking was also an issue.

In 2013, Roger Brown bought the company for $9 million from the estate of Heselden and on April 1, 2015, he sold it to a Chinese transportation robotics startup called Ninebot for $75 million. Now one of the two largest scooter manufacturers in the world, they are the supplier for Bird and Lime, and their scooters are used in more than 100 cities all over the world. This success can be explained by a realignment along the A1 axis:

- **PERCEPTION.** It's okay to ride a scooter. All the kids use them and it's not unusual to see parents taking their kids to school on one. It's not perceived as geeky.

- **PRICE.** Rentals are cheap and can be conveniently managed from my smartphone.

- **SAFETY.** They are perceived to be safe when used with a helmet. I don't have to learn how to use them and figure out how to turn, accelerate or stop by shifting the weight of my body.

- **CONVENIENCE.** I can ride and park them pretty much anywhere, like a bicycle.

It seems like the last-mile issue has found a viable solution and the Pain versus Claim alignment has been largely addressed.

WHAT WE HAVE LEARNED

➤ The first axis of alignment is Pain ⟷ Claim. The pain the person or the organization experiences and the claim the business makes have to be aligned for a transaction to be even possible.

➤ Pain can be latent and becomes explicit (expressed) once a legitimate claim has been made.

➤ In some cases, it is the fear of missing out that constitute the pain. I define this phenomenon as the "Pain of Negation."

➤ The amount of pain, the urgency to solve it and the current coping mechanism will determine the level of desire to solve it and ultimately the size of the market addressing that pain.

➤ The awareness of the claim (i.e. the existence of a potential cure to the pain) to potential customers (i.e. people or organizations that constitute the affinity market) is one of the key drivers of revenue growth. Businesses must find a cost-effective way to express and communicate their claim when they first introduce it.

➤ A claim cannot be made without a price (yes, it can be free). Pricing optimization for each target segment insures maximum revenue generation.

➤ Misalignment between pain and claim decreases the opportunity for a transaction and therefore negatively affects revenue growth.

CASE STUDIES

➤ Aperture Investors: a good pricing alignment

➤ Levi Strauss & Co: a solid A1 alignment

➤ Segway: a dramatic A1 misalignment

NEXT CHAPTER

➤ Focuses on A2, the second axis of alignment: Perception versus Message.

66

A great brand is a story that
never stops unfolding.

TONY HSIEH
CEO of Zappos.com

SECOND AXIS

Perception versus Message

ALIGNMENT AXES	CUSTOMER		BUSINESS	GOAL
1	Pain	→ | ←	Claim	Real painkiller
2	Perception	→ | ←	Message	Compelling story
3	Purchase	→ | ←	Sale	Frictionless transaction
4	Delight	→ | ←	Offering	Insane delight

The second axis of alignment in the *A4 Precision Alignment*™ methodology focuses on what a prospect perceives about a company, product or service, versus the message being communicated to that prospect. The concept: if prospects don't understand the Claim, even though it may be 100% aligned with their Pain, they simply won't buy the product.

Remember Sylvia, who could not understand the pharmacist who was speaking to her in Korean?

This is really all about positioning, which, as so eloquently stated by Boone and Kurtz, is about "the placement of the product in the minds of prospective customers"[7] so that the image of the claim becomes imprinted in the brain of the consumers. It's about the perception of the product, what it does, how it addresses the pain and, finally, why a prospect should care. **This is why defining and controlling that perception is critical, as it takes a lot of energy, time and money to change a perception when it is not imprinted correctly.**

The critical role of precision segmentation

An important aspect of the A2 alignment is prospect segmentation. The message and the method for delivering that message have to be adapted and mapped depending on which market segment is pursued. With his landmark book *Crossing the Chasm,* Geoffrey Moore taught us that companies have to convince a succession of different types of prospects to successfully reach large-scale, mainstream customers. While written close to 30 years ago, Moore's book is still incredibly relevant today.

In his book *Market Segmentation: A Step-By-Step Guide to Profitable New Business,* Michael Croft defines market segmentation as "the process of identifying different groups of users within a market who could possibly be targeted with separate products or marketing programs". There's an even more relevant aspect to this today, with the idea of social groups where segments of customers are organized in accessible online communities.

Once the company has understood and defined its affinity market, the next step is to build a segmentation framework. This is done by defining a taxonomy by which prospects can be put in various MECE (mutually exclusive, collectively exclusive) buckets. Sorting can be based on attributes such as their size, their propensity to adopt new technology, demographic attributes (for example, age or gender), vertical or industry they belong to, business geographic footprint, online conversations/online cross-over patterns based on user-generated content, etc.

---

7   Boone and Kurtz, from the 2009 edition of *Contemporary Marketing*, page 303.

Precision segmentation is important because the way the claim is expressed will need to be fine-tuned to the specific targeted segment. It encompasses the message itself, but also the types of advertising and marketing programs to reach that segment. It also helps identify which segments can be satisfied most effectively and profitably. In other words, it helps focus.

For example, in an article titled "Mini Coopers: Marketing Strategy, Digital Marketing, Brand and Ethics," Mariia Moiseieva explained, "Mini's marketing strategy has shifted from marketing an icon to marketing an iconic cool luxury car for a young segment." Clearly the framework by which Mini has segmented its affinity market has evolved over time and has become more precisely defined.

Tell me in one sentence: why I should I buy your product?

Over the past three decades, as a venture capitalist, I have met more than 2,500 CEOs. For a long time, I used to ask them the same question: "What does your company do?" They love that question. They get it all the time, at cocktail parties, on business trips or at school events. I'd sit down by a CEO I'd never met before and pose the question.

After a while, I realized I was asking the wrong question. The answer invariably tends to be a long monologue about how great whatever they do is, how revolutionary and new it is and how it will change the world forever. I call that the "Wanting-to-Make-the-Planet-Spin-the-Other-Way" response.

So, I decided to not ask the "What does your company do?" question anymore. I now ask a different one. A very different question indeed. Interestingly, it gives many CEOs pause. The question is: "Don't tell me what your company does. Instead, tell me in one sentence why should I buy your product?" A strong CEO should be able to answer this question quickly, intelligently and crisply.

Sometimes, however, I'm surprised by the answer. I remember the early days of WebTV Networks, a company started by Steve Perlman that developed a combination of hardware, software and services. The hardware was a device that plugged into a TV and a phone jack. It enabled that TV to receive content from the internet (yes, via an old plain RJ11 telephone connection). It offered many functionalities of the computer, such as web browsing, email, and rich content. Steve described his company as "a way of bringing computers to average people," which in July 1995, when the company started, was no small feat. The product was launched in September the following year. Only 22 months after the company was founded, Microsoft acquired it for a whopping $425 million. It was a big deal, since WebTV was both the very first company to have a TV connected to the internet and the first to have a consumer device (as opposed to a computer) access the Web. In a way, it was the Internet of Things (IoT) way ahead of its time. Steve and his team had a clear answer to the "why" question: bringing computers to average people. This was transformative indeed.

The "why" question centers the discussion on the claim and what compels a person to decide to give money in exchange for the product or service. It is not about the "what" or the "how" but the "why." Larry King used to say that his favorite question was "Why?" It's an open-ended question, and the answer can be surprising and often leads to other questions and a more engaging and fruitful discussion.

When asked the "Why should I buy?" question, the first logical thought the CEO should have is "Are you a potential customer?" Maybe the answer is "You should never buy my product because I sell complex equipment for manufacturing MRI medical machines and I am ready to bet my next paycheck that you will never buy my $15 million machine." Kidding aside, any CEO should have a solid answer to this simple question.

I recently talked to Armand Thiberge, the co-founder and CEO of SendinBlue, a marketing automation company delivering "Marketing Campaigns Made Easy." Thiberge is a brilliant entrepreneur who raised a whopping $36 million Series A venture round in September 2017, led by Partech. Shortly thereafter, the company claimed 50,000 customers, sending over 30 million emails every day. Yes, that's close to 11 billion emails per year! I asked Thiberge my favorite question and his answer still resonates with me: "We provide an email marketing platform to SMBs [small and medium-sized businesses] that's easy to use and cheap. We compete against other offerings like Constant Contact, Emma, MailChimp, SendGrid and others, but we are ten times cheaper. This is why you should buy!" That was a powerful answer. First off, he was able to describe what SendinBlue does in three words, "email marketing platform." Next, he understands his top competitors and is not afraid of them. Finally, the answer to the "why" was very crisp: it is simply ten times cheaper.

Give it a try. Pose the "why" question to CEOs and see what they tell you. I bet it will be a much more interesting discussion than the long monologue you have heard so many times.

The cause

Having a cause, a Point-of-View (POV), belief or conviction brings clarity to the "Why should I buy?" question. **The reason a company does what it does profoundly matters.** As Simon Sinek so eloquently explained in his TED Talk about The Golden Circles and Start with Why, people don't buy what you do, they buy why you do it.

As Sinek pointed out, in his infamous speech during the march on Washington for Jobs and Freedom on August 28, 1963, Martin Luther King Jr. did not proclaim, "I have a plan." This would not have been uplifting. Instead, he told the 250,000 civil rights supporters from the steps of the Lincoln Memorial, "I have a dream." The dream is the "Why"; the plan is the "What." Most don't care about the "What."

When I met with Phillip Dunkelberger, who was the CEO of PGP (Pretty Good Privacy), to discuss this book, he told me an interesting story. Early in his career, he had the opportunity to meet with Don Lucas. Don was one of the early and renowned godfathers of the venture capital industry, along with John Doerr, Don Valentine, Tom Perkins and General William H. Draper Jr. Don Lucas asked Dunkelberger a question that stuck in his mind: "Do you want to be on the cover of *Wired Magazine* or do you want to change the world?" Dunkelberger went on to explain to me that to build a real business, you have to be driven by a mission and dream about it constantly. PGP was acquired in 2010 by Symantec in a deal valued at $324 million.

The farsighted book *Play Bigger: How Pirates, Dreamers, and Innovators Create and Dominate Markets* makes the case that dominant companies, the ones that win and take the leadership position in a market, are the ones that have a different POV. They become category leaders. The book was authored by four veteran Silicon Valley entrepreneurs: Al Ramadan (I first met Ramadan in 1999, when he was the CEO of Quokka Sports, one of our portfolio companies, at Allegis Capital), Dave Peterson, Christopher Lochhead and Kevin Maney, a veteran technology journalist. Category winners are not better than their competitors; they are different. The book is based on what the authors call Category Design. Examples covered in the book are companies such as 5-hour ENERGY, Amazon, Facebook, IKEA, Netflix, Salesforce, SpaceX and Uber. It's not about beating the competition. **It's about creating a whole new category.** Category creation is the new grail, not disruption. Explaining why they are different is the message and the ultimate expression of the claim.

Here are a few examples of stated missions:

COMPANY	POINT OF VIEW
Airbnb	"Live in the world where one day you can feel like you're home anywhere and not in a home, but truly home, where you belong."
Amazon	"Be earth's most customer-centric company; to build a place where people can come to find and discover anything they might want to buy online."
Google	"To organize the world's information and make it universally accessible and useful."
Tesla	"Accelerate the advent of sustainable transport by bringing compelling mass market electric cars to market as soon as possible."
Twitter	"Give everyone the power to create and share ideas and information instantly, without barriers."
Uber	"Make transportation as reliable as running water, everywhere, for everyone."

Point-of-view examples

The common theme among all these successful companies is about being different, not simply being better, and having a strong, bold and well-stated POV.

Claim and trust as yin and yang

If a clear answer to the "Why" question is the first critical concept at the core of the A2 alignment, the second one is *trust*.

One of the most painful outcomes for a business is when a person or a company makes the decision not to buy a product, not because it's not the right product at the right price, but because they did not understand the product, its value, the cost structure or how it would address their pain and make their lives better.

Imagine you are in the market to purchase new health insurance and no one is able to clearly articulate a pricing structure for the insurance. Will the insurance reimburse the particular medicine I need for my condition? How much of that cost am I liable for up front? Will it impact my deductible? How long will the insurance company take to reimburse my out-of-pocket expenses? Do I have to see the doctor again to get refills or do I simply pay the co-payment every time I need a refill? A good health-care insurance company is able to answer each of these legitimate questions with clarity and speed[8].

Trust is also set by the language. If I am looking for new skydiving gear and the company does not speak the skydiving lingo, would I buy? No, no way! People selling skydiving equipment have done hundreds, if not thousands, of jumps. First, the salesperson will want to know how many jumps you have. Then, he will ask if you want an AAD (automated activation device). He will inquire about the type of main canopy and the size you want: 7-cell, 9-cell, F111, ZP, Hybrid, low bulk, square, semi-elliptical, elliptical, air-locked, cross-braced, etc., as there are many types. Due to the nature of his questions and the vocabulary he is using, you trust the person's expertise right away. You understand that he knows what he's talking about and can articulate trade-offs. In exchange, you grant him your trust.

A good message is delivered in a way that establishes an uncompromised trust.

Trust is a required condition to making the decision to buy. Often, the message is the first thing you hear about a product or service. It's the first impression. If I don't understand what the person is talking about or

---

8   Although a good insurance company (according to economists Thaler and Sunstein in their book *Nudge*) gets the default option right, as most people do not ask the important questions up front and select the default options.

connect with it at an emotional level, then it will be an uphill battle for me to buy. Oftentimes, brand equity is a source of trust that can be leveraged in a new business or new product offering. Would you invest in a new company started by Marc Benioff or Barry Diller? Bill Gates or Elon Musk? How about Elizabeth Holmes?

The easiest way to realign along the A2 axis

It is much harder to change the Perception than it is to change the Message. Companies need to thoroughly understand the importance of setting the right message in the first place. This process has to be controlled by the business, not by competition, the press or channel partners and certainly not by customers. The tone, the words, the language and the sophistication of the content are all-important components of the message and must always be under the control of the company.

This is what Bob Wright, founder and managing director of Firebrick Consulting, describes as "Differentiate or Die." He explains that the true game-changers are very clear about why buyers should buy and at answering the following three questions:

1. How are you different?

2. Why your product now?

3. How will you make your buyer's life better?

The message can be as simple as "The Ultimate Driving Machine," which captures the essence of the claim for BMW, or as complicated and as nebulous as "IBM's suite of enterprise-ready AI services, applications and tooling" for Watson, the computer system that can answer questions posed in natural language.

While the essence of the claim cannot be altered because it has to be truthful, the content of the message has to be an honest and authentic interpretation of that claim and it must resonate with the type of prospects targeted. **The goal is to express the claim in a way that is understood by the target prospect and at the same time, inspires confidence and trust.** Once the perception has been set, it is very hard to alter it. It is a lot easier to carefully refine the message until it is perfect, after it has been deliberately tested with the right target audience.

A stunning example of redefining a company

A few years ago, a young CEO named Rena came to me with an interesting business. She was preparing and delivering lunches for busy workers. Her idea was simple: lunch on demand, when and where you need it. Think about this common scenario. It's lunchtime and you're in a meeting with seven of your colleagues, in the middle of an intense strategy planning discussion for next fiscal year, and everyone is hungry. It was supposed to be a one-hour meeting, but the discussion took on a life of its own. No plans have been made for lunch, and everyone wants to bring the discussion to a conclusion and hopefully make one or two important decisions before the meeting wraps up. What are your options?

At the time, there were a number of companies delivering food at business locations, including:

- Seamless (raised over $50 million in venture money);

- Grubhub (raised over $190 million before going public in April 2014, and previously merged with Seamless in May of 2013);

- Eat24 (acquired by Grubhub in August 2017 for close to $300 million);

- DoorDash (raised close to $200 million in venture money from prominent VC firms like Kleiner Perkins Caufield & Byers, Sequoia Capital, Khosla Ventures and Y Combinator);

- OrderUp (acquired by Groupon in July 2015 after raising $10 million in venture money);

- other large brand companies that were also entering the space, such as Uber (with the Uber Eats app), Yelp (bought Food24 for $134 million in February 2015) and Amazon, with a service called Amazon Restaurants and more anticipated in the future from their Whole Foods acquisition;

- and many other startups, competing for the same market.

All these companies were focused on delivering food and meals through what they claimed to be an amazing mobile app experience with ease-of-ordering, seamless payment, tracking, logistics and availability to deliver to remote locations. In a way, they wanted to change the experience of ordering and consuming food for busy employees.

Rena's company was no different, but one thing caught my attention: she was focused on delivering healthy food. Rena built her business on the notion that eating at a desk or in a conference room was no excuse to not enjoy healthy food. Two things drove her: delivering the healthiest possible food at a reasonable price, and preserving the planet by respecting the environment. Ingredients were fresh and organic; meals were prepared from scratch every single day. The packaging was not only beautiful but was carefully chosen to be environmentally friendly with biodegradable material.

Customers were enthused by the quality of the food and the idea that they contributed to keeping the planet clean and the environment safe. The very first time I met Rena, I was impressed by her passion and enthusiasm. When I asked her what business she was in, she simply answered, "We prepare and deliver good food to busy workers." Her business model was to sell through HR departments of large companies, relying on them to promote her food services internally. Unfortunately, she was banging her head against the wall of competitors that were offering similar services.

After several discussions with Rena, it finally hit me. I realized that she was in the wrong business. One day, as we met for coffee, I told her, "You are in the wrong business. You are NOT in the food delivery business." She was shocked and replied, "Of course we are. That's what we do." I pushed back and said, "No, this is not the business you are in." She asked, "So, what business are we in?" My response was simple and shocking to her: "You are in the business of prolonging life."

"How so?" she asked. My view was straightforward: no one would argue against the idea that eating healthy makes people live longer. There is a huge volume of medical literature demonstrating how consuming unhealthy food creates all kinds of health issues. Rena realized I was right.

So, the idea was to change the pitch to the HR person and say, "I am here to make your employees happier, healthier, have a more balanced life and above all, live longer. Are you interested in hearing more?" She then went on to explain how the organic ingredients were chosen; how a nutritionist, who was part of her team, carefully planned balanced, healthy meals; and how much she and her team cared about the environment. She even printed a list of all her major competitors with links to their websites, explaining, "If you prefer your employees to eat less healthy food, live shorter lives and add to the destruction of our precious planet, here is a list of companies with great offers."

I also argued that company employees should pay even more than what her competitors were charging. The tongue-in-cheek message was: "Wouldn't you be willing to pay a little extra to live longer?" or "How much would you pay for each extra month of a healthy life?"

By changing the message and realigning the company along the A2 axis, we accomplished two things:

1. We created a real, differentiated message and wrote new rules completely different from the ones our competitors followed. We are all about prolonging life, not delivering food at lunchtime to busy and hungry workers.

2. We could easily justify a higher price. This is one of the easiest ways to grow revenue, as explained in Chapter 3. Price was increased by 15% with pretty much no pushback.

The important point is that Rena did not need to change her product in any way. She changed the message, the way the claim was articulated. It is a lot easier, faster and cheaper to change the message than the product.

DAITAN

A successful realignment along the second axis

Shortly after starting Blue Dots, we worked on a project for one of our clients, a Silicon Valley company called Daitan. The company offers near-shore outsourcing software development services from Canada and Brazil for large and midsize corporations. The quality of the code they wrote was high and the way they were implementing their client projects was well conceived and managed by highly trained software development managers.

Using Blue Dots' disciplined, data-driven approach (described in detail in Chapter 8), we carefully crafted a short, 12-question interview guide that was approved by our client CEO. Our goal was to talk to 36 Daitan customers, and we started to make calls.

One of the open-ended questions we asked was: "Can you describe in one sentence the value you received?"

The answer was a big surprise to us.

Daitan had initially explained to us that their value was to offer top-quality software engineering services at a lower cost than Silicon valley. In essence, the value was good quality at a low cost. According to data released by Glassdoor in September 2018, the average annual base pay for a software engineer in the San Francisco Bay Area is $137,000 (19% above national average) plus $11,000 additional cash compensation. The fully loaded cost of that engineer, including medical benefits, 401(k) plan and all kinds of perks, including, in some cases, the ability to play Ping-Pong at 9 p.m., is about $190,000. Our client would, at the time, offer a team of experienced software developers, fully dedicated to the project, with typically eight years of experience building real products, for around $80,000 per year. Since the engineers are contracting with our client, there are no employee liabilities or additional employer tax, Workers' Compensation, medical benefits, 401(k) plan, stock option plan or other costs. One would think that a 3-times price difference was a great deal of value.

What we heard from the interviews we did with Daitan's customers was quite different. Indeed, they told us that the value for them was time-to-market. Most of them have a very hard time recruiting quality software developers and retaining them, especially in highly competitive markets like the Bay Area, Seattle, Los Angeles, New York City or Denver. For example, in the Bay Area, it is very hard to recruit the best engineers when Facebook, Google, Twitter, Apple and Tesla are all fighting for them. In the Seattle area, it is hard to convince a 23-year-old AI software developer to not work for Microsoft or Amazon and join a team of 35 employees who want to create the next Unicorn and have barely raised $1.5 million in seed financing.

On the other hand, the cost for a company to delay releasing a fully tested new product because they are behind on their engineering hiring plan is very high, especially for VC- backed companies where the pressure to ship the product and start generating "real" revenue is tremendous. In fact, we discovered via our interview process that companies would be willing to pay a premium to have these resources faster, because the cost of missing a deadline to launch a product is real and significant. On top of that, there's the PR headache of explaining that the next version of the product will now ship in July instead of Q1 as was announced last year or that you've missed a promised launch at the Consumer Electronics Show (CES) or another trade conference. In other words, time-to-market was the real value, not cost savings.

So, we repositioned the company messaging to "Accelerate" and advised Daitan to increase their pricing. The pitch became: "If you are looking for cheap software developers, that's not us. If you are looking for dependable, well-trained and experienced developers who will help you ship on time, then let's have a conversation."

The new positioning was not about cost or money, but about time. That insight came when we interviewed Daitan's customers and asked, "How much would you be willing to pay to engage one specific engineer one week earlier? One month earlier?" The answers we received validated that time-to-market was the key driver of the purchase decision, not cost reduction.

This illustrates how changing the expression of the claim made a huge difference. It is a lot easier to do it this way than the other way around, which is to change the product or services. It is very effective, often overlooked and much cheaper.

HEALTH IQ

A healthy A2 alignment

Here is the case of another company that, in my opinion, has realized a good A2 alignment.

In 2013, a team of nine entrepreneurs started a company in the heart of Silicon Valley called Health IQ. The company has a strong mission statement: to increase the world's health literacy, which has been lagging behind the world's language literacy. Through three rounds of financing, the company raised over $80 million in venture money from some of the best VC firms in the Valley.

A serial entrepreneur, CEO Munjal Shah, explained to me, "My team and I have worked for years to celebrate the health-conscious with financial rewards." His health conscientiousness was triggered by a trip to the ER after experiencing chest pain while running a 10K race. Health IQ's go-to-market strategy came together after realizing that insurance companies were willing to charge less to health-conscious people, since the statistics show that they tend to live healthier and longer lives. It's akin to a car insurance company charging less for an experienced driver with a clean record. The epiphany to Shah and his team was that there was an opportunity to become the first company to address the market of health-conscious consumers.

Health IQ launched their first product, life insurance for health-conscious people, in March 2016. Almost three years later, in January 2019, the company had secured life policies for over $15 billion in total coverage. They are a licensed broker in all 50 states and have underwritten life insurance policies for thousands of people. They work with highly rated carriers such as Ameritas, John Hancock, Lincoln Financial Group, Mutual of Omaha, New York Life, Principal, Prudential, SBLI and Transamerica.

The company has enjoyed an impressive growth in coverage, as exhibited in the chart below:

CASE STUDY

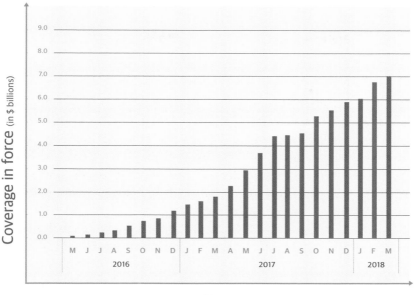

Health IQ insurance coverage
(Source: Health IQ website)

The product is designed for health-conscious people in general and is particularly appealing to athletes such as runners, swimmers, cyclists, weightlifters, triathletes and HIIT (high-intensity interval trainers), as well as yogis and vegans. The Health IQ website is full of research content and statistics. Results of scientific studies hammer home the point that health-conscious people are healthier and live longer and because of that, should be paying lower life insurance premiums than the rest of the population.

So, how are the two axes of alignment realized in this example?

- **PAIN:** You have to pay the same for life insurance as people who are not as health-conscious as you are.

- **CLAIM:** You should be rewarded for your health-consciousness: we save you money because you are lower risk.

- **MESSAGE:** Four reasons why health-conscious consumers should get a lower rate on life insurance.

- **PERCEPTION:** I am health-conscious and understand why I should pay less.

The A2 alignment in this case is clear. It takes me one minute to fill out a quick form to get a free quote, and then an agent calls me within 24 hours. Health IQ has enjoyed great success in building its business and is on track to generate close to $100 million in revenue in less than six years.

HALO TOP

Ice cream with no remorse

Another good example of a solid A2 alignment is Halo Top.

The company was founded in June 2012 by Justin Woolverton, a former lawyer who was subject to hypoglycemic diet restrictions. His main idea was to offer "lifestyle" ice creams that are both healthy and made with all-natural ingredients. The 25 flavors they offer today are low-calorie, high-protein and low-sugar, but they actually taste like regular ice creams. The claim about being healthy is well expressed (good A2 alignment) and is backed by clear facts:

	HALO TOP	HÄAGEN DAZS	BEN & JERRY'S	DREYER'S SLOW CHURNED
Calories	60	250	250	100
Protein	5g	5g	4g	3g
Fat	2g	2g	16g	3g
Carbs	5g	5g	21g	15g

Halo Top comparison to its top competitors

Remarkably, in July 2017, Halo Top became the best-selling ice cream in grocery stores, displacing both Ben & Jerry's and Häagen-Dazs, who had enjoyed that distinction for many years. Today, Halo Top is continuing to build a strong base of devoted fans who embrace the company's claim, and the company enjoys solid growth in its business.

NEWTON

A perfect A2 misalignment

Apple does not always get it right. Here is an illustration of a disastrous A2 misalignment in the making.

Newton, "the first personal digital assistant," officially called MessagePad, was launched by Apple's CEO John Sculley on May 29, 1992 during the CES show in Chicago. It was released on August 2, 1993 with a base price of $699.99. It shipped with Names, a contact database; Notes, a handwriting application to draw sketches and write notes; and Dates, a calendar.

Steve Capps, chief architect of Newton, who previously co-developed the Finder, the file system for the Mac, explained, "The goals were to design a new category of handheld device and to build a platform to support it."

From the get-go, confusion around the device was high. Apple failed to explain how the product would be used or why someone should fork over $700 to buy one. Was it:

- A game console?
- A substitute for a computer?
- A PIM (personal information manager) for the traveler?
- An electronic notebook for busy mothers to jot notes?
- A communication device to help people keep in touch?
- An easy way to fax? (No, I did not make that up!)
- A way to share information from one device to another?
- An intelligent assistant to help me do what I want to do?

Apple ran a series of ads to illustrate the variety of applications for the new device, but they caused more confusion in the market. The fundamental issue was that people did not understand Newton and didn't know what to do with it. In other words, they did not know "Why" they should buy the device or what pain the device would address. One of the ads started with a sensible question: "What is Newton?" and went on by answering: "Newton is digital. Newton is personal. Newton is magic. Newton is as powerful as a computer and as simple as a piece of paper. Newton is intelligent." If this doesn't confuse you, then I don't know what would! There is no emotional connection, no answer to the "Why should I buy" question. It did not trigger a strong desire or impulse to buy. I'm not motivated to stand in line just to get my hands on it. No benefits were described. It might have been better if the ad explained what Newton is not. Another ad says it all: "Newton is about a lot of things. Really."

To confuse things even further, Apple released seven models over a six-year period.

In the end, only 300,000 units were sold during the 4.5 years Newton was on the market, despite a rock-solid loyal and fervent Mac user base. The new product was not perceived as a complementary or substitute product. Also, uncharacteristically of Apple, the company shared way too much information about an immature project, first talking about the concept in 1991 and then rushing to release the product two years later with a significant number of deficits. Apple over-promised with its pre-launch buildup, creating unrealistic market expectations that naturally resulted in massive disappointment. Users were not willing to spend $700 for a product they simply could not understand. Newton became a "beautiful failure." The perception of the product and its value was not aligned with the myriad unmet claims Apple made. It was a clear case of a total and embarrassing A2 misalignment at scale.

WHAT WE HAVE LEARNED

➤ The second axis of alignment is Perception ⟷ Message.

➤ The perception, which is the understanding of the claim, and the expression of that claim have to be aligned for a transaction to be possible.

➤ There are two core enablers of the A2 alignment:

   1. A clear answer to the "Why should I buy" question

   2. The establishment of trust, because trust is the foundation for validating that the claim is credible and for securing.

➤ Precision market segmentation has to be well defined. A2 alignment is a function of knowing who the target customer is and using their own language to express their pain.

➤ Positioning and messaging must be crafted carefully and succinctly and appeal at an emotional level.

➤ Getting the message right in the first place is a lot easier, faster and cheaper than changing the Perception once it's set in the mind of the consumer.

➤ Misalignment between perception and message decreases the opportunity for a transaction and therefore negatively affects revenue growth.

CASE STUDIES

➤ Daitan: a successful realignment along the second axis

➤ Health IQ: a healthy A2 alignment

➤ Halo Top: Ice cream with no remorse

➤ Newton: a perfect A2 misalignment

NEXT CHAPTER

➤ Introduces A3, the third axis of alignment: Purchase versus Sale.

66

The reality is that the challenge
is to transition sales from
an art form to a science.

PHIL DUNKELBERGER
President and CEO at Nok Nok Labs

THIRD AXIS

Purchase versus Sale

ALIGNMENT AXES	CUSTOMER		BUSINESS	GOAL
1	Pain	→ | ←	Claim	Real painkiller
2	Perception	→ | ←	Message	Compelling story
3	Purchase	→ | ←	Sale	Frictionless transaction
4	Delight	→ | ←	Offering	Insane delight

The third axis of the *A4 Precision Alignment™* methodology only material-izes when the decision to purchase the product or service has been made. As we described in Chapter 4, the first axis is a function of awareness of both a Pain and the existence of a Claim. Chapter 5 focuses on the second axis, the Perception versus the Message. This is the phase where the pros-pect is becoming convinced to buy the product or service and establishing that there is a good fit. The next phase is to actually go through the process of buying the product or service. I define this as the modality of acquisition.

The "second" product must be how to sell the first

A mistake commonly made after the first product or service is launched is to rush into building the next product. We see it in the software industry with an accelerating pace of cranking out new features and new products, and sometimes even launching several products at the same time, creating total confusion. Here are a few examples:

- On September 12, 2017, Apple announced its new iPhone 8 as "An all new glass design. The world's most popular camera, now even better. The most powerful and smartest chip ever in a smartphone. Wireless charging that's truly effortless. And augmented reality experiences never before possible. iPhone 8. A new generation of iPhone." Now, about half an hour later, Apple's CEO Tim Cook unveiled the real new iPhone: the iPhone X. Here is how is was described on Apple's website: "Our vision has always been to create an iPhone that is entirely screen. One so immersive the device itself disappears into the experience. And so intelligent it can respond to a tap, your voice, and even a glance. With iPhone X, that vision is now a reality. Say hello to the future." Of course, that was among a number of other products and services announced at the same time. History repeated itself on September 12, 2018, with the announcement of not two, but three new iPhone models: the iPhone XR, the iPhone XS and iPhone XS Max!

- On March 31, 2016, Elon Musk announced the Tesla Model 3. After two and a half years, countless production delays and issues with the battery pack manufacturing, the car still wasn't available for a test drive. There were more than 400,000 people on the waiting list with no clear timing for delivery. On top of that, on November 16, 2017, Musk unveiled Tesla Semi, his new electric freight truck. Toward the end of the presentation, Musk had another trick up his sleeve: he added (yes, I chose the word "added" carefully here) a beautiful roadster, reminiscent of the very first car Tesla ever built. He did it by taking a page out of

Apple's playbook to wow the crowd. The production of the truck is expected to begin in 2019 and the roadster, which will cost $200,000, sometime in 2020. I could not help but wonder how people who placed an order almost two years ago for a Model 3 felt about this.

What I call the "second product" for a company has nothing to do with a real, tangible product. **It's all about how the product is sold. It's the Go-to-Market (GTM) plan.** Indeed, the process and mechanism of selling needs to be approached in the same rigorous way as designing and building a product. A typical product engineering process starts with a point of view, some hypothesis, ideas, a concept, followed by assembling a team of high-quality engineers, scientists, UX and UI artists, developing specifications, crafting a development plan, putting together test cases and scripts for Q&A, writing documentation, preparing packaging, etc.

The GTM ought to follow the same discipline: it starts with the GTM specs. What's the plan? Which market segments will we go after? What geographies should we focus on initially? What are the detailed steps or sequences in the marketing process to acquire qualified leads and in the sales process to convert them?

Here is an example of a plan for that second product: The goal is to figure out, fairly quickly and efficiently, a repeatable "sales factory" process; in other words, how the sales flywheel works from lead qualification to closing the sale (i.e. signing the agreement for business). These are the subsequent challenges that need to be addressed:

1. Define who we truly are, what our unique value is; establish a point of view, a mission and a purpose.

2. Conduct a precision segmentation exercise for the affinity market and the persona we want to target (a representation of your ideal customer) and prioritize them.

3. Articulate the problem statement in a way that any prospect who has that pain will quickly and clearly resonate with it and acknowledge it. This needs to be tested and refined, starting with current customers.

4. Express our claim. The key here is to not explain our features, but *only* our benefits. Remember, people buy the "why," not the "what." If a specific feature does not translate into a clear and

tangible benefit, then it should not be brought up (to be blunt, who cares?).

5. Put together various messages for prospect communication (email, LinkedIn message, website, video, testimonials, white papers, industry-leading communication, etc.).

6. Develop sales sequences with key tracking metrics and conduct A/B testing to see which ones deliver the best results, i.e. have the highest conversion rate.

7. Test and finalize the lead generation process for both outbound and inbound campaigns.

8. Develop the sales playbook to convert. It will be used for training and memorializing the entire process, its metrics and rationale.

The "Experiential Journey"

Here's a new phenomenon, just happening! Brands and businesses are finally starting to understand that their customers are a lot more than human beings with credit cards or the power to sign a PO (purchase order). Not just someone ranting on an email that he or she has not received the product ordered on the internet a few days ago. It is no longer about an order number, a complex alphanumeric chain for a support ticket or an SKU number for a particular size and color pair of shoes.

It's now all about establishing an emotional relationship with each customer. Connection and empathy. Emotion. Brands such as Apple, Nike, Southwest Airlines, Starbucks, Tesla, Zappos and others have recognized and embraced that notion. It is imprinted in their DNA. They put customers first and value their various interactions with them through what I call the *Experiential Journey*. Rather than a succession of disconnected interaction points, it's a journey with the profound goal of establishing and nurturing a lasting emotional bond with the customer. This is also true in business-to-business relationships where the purchaser feels respected, heard and valued. It feels more like a partnership than a vendor/supplier relationship.

We sometimes witness this phenomenon in small stores or restaurants. The owner knows you, knows what you like and dislike, your tastes and habits. She calls you by your first name and knows your spouse's name too. This is how grocery stores used to be decades ago. They knew their customers so well that they didn't hesitate to give them credit and charge them later. Now, when you walk into a Home Depot, nobody knows you. Sometimes, it's even hard to know who works there and can help you. Sometimes there is no associate in sight, except the cashier with a line of eight people waiting with growing impatience. With no name or identity, you're just a purchase transaction waiting to happen.

Selling a product to a consumer can no longer be reduced to merely a transaction or a series of cold and sometimes contentious support calls. **It has to be a journey, based on a story.** In fact, it's a two-way storytelling where both parties actively participate and engage. The internet and mobile devices are leveling the playing field. A small company, located just about anywhere, can now give pause and grief to the most powerful brands by putting the customer right in the center of the experiential journey. It starts with grabbing her attention, delighting her so much that she tells all her friends on Facebook and Instagram. She now becomes an active protagonist in telling the story on her own terms. She becomes an important brand ambassador. It's a two-way relationship, which is a lot more powerful than the one-to-many directional approach traditionally used in mass advertising. This is true for support as well. As J.D. Power indicated, 67% of consumers have used a company's social media site for service.

In the July/August 2017 issue of *Inc.* magazine, Steph Korey, the co-founder of Away, explained it well: "Storytelling is a central part of our marketing. We think about what stories we can feed to the press and to social media. Things that make people notice, things people want to share and talk about." Her company grew to $12 million in sales in one year.

Understanding the customer also means understanding the relevant dimensions that enable a connection with each customer. For example, it can be an inflection point in their life: your customer could be a woman who just had a baby, a student starting college or a family moving across the country. Another dimension can be the cadence and rhythm of buying. If I have a hot tub, then I need to buy chemicals periodically to keep my tub balanced. If I wear lenses, I need a new pair every so often. The connection can be seasonal, such as buying particular fresh ingredients for a holiday or celebration, or needing to prune the trees in my garden.

The third eCommerce revolution and the DTC economy

Over the past few years, online commerce has changed radically. I believe we are now in the third eCommerce revolution. The first started in July 1994, when Jeff Bezos founded Amazon in his garage. The second was in June 2007, when Steve Jobs introduced the iPhone and started the mobile commerce revolution. The third one is what I call *Personalized Commerce*. It is based on the notion that there is no reason why two different people should see the exact same eCommerce site. Merchandizing, product accessibility and availability, shipping time, discount offerings and even pricing should vary from one shopper to the next based on personal tastes, past history and other personal traits. Big data, artificial intelligence (AI) and machine learning are beginning to fuel that revolution.

We now see the emergence of the direct-to-consumer (DTC) movement. It's sometimes called the *Direct Brand Economy*. It's the consumer economy where, via social media, the power is shifting from brands to consumers.

Historically, supply chain dominance was a good proxy for market dominance. Whoever controlled the supply chain controlled the market. While this continues to be an important asset, it has started to erode over the past few years.

The battle is no longer at the merchandizing and supply chain level; the battle is fought at the data level. Whoever owns the data and understands how to extract insights, signals and predictive behavior is going to win. No longer are location, square footage, signage, media coverage or shelf arrangement the weapons dictating who wins and who loses on the commerce battlefield. The modern weapons are redirecting, capturing abandoned shopping carts, personalized email drop campaigns and social media engagement. What used to take months for a launch program now takes minutes. The supply chain is being turned on its head. It's all about efficiency, nimbleness and responding to each customer's expectations and demands. New business models are emerging for on-demand and subscription-based as well as second-hand products.

Distance and time are being dramatically compressed: people want same-day (sometimes same-hour) delivery. Over 83% of BOPUS (buy online, pick up in store) customers expect to pick up their order in less than 24 hours. In this case, they will sacrifice distance for time. Conversely, the success of Amazon shows that many consumers want home delivery, preferring not to drive the distance back and forth to a retail store.

In a July 2017 article, *Time* stated that more than 8,600 retail stores could close in the US that year, including 5,300 JCPenney, Kmart, Macy's and Sears stores that had already shuttered. Large brands are suffering from slow or negative growth. It is stunning to realize that on October 15, 2018, Sears filed for bankruptcy protection. The company was America's preeminent retailer and sixth-largest stock 50 years ago. According to the IAB report *The Rise of the 21st Century Brand Economy,* the FMCG (fast-moving consumer goods) industry grew only 1% in 2017 as revenue shifted to new channels and new categories. This is affecting revenue growth for iconic brands such as Coca-Cola, General Mills, Kellogg's, Kraft Heinz, P&G, PepsiCo and Unilever. The same report explains that the direct economy contributed 6% of the GDP in 2016 ($1.1 billion), which was much higher than the 3.7% in 2012 ($300 million).

Previously unknown online DTC brands, in various categories, are now becoming a real threat to large, established brands:

CATEGORY	INCUMBENTS	UPCOMERS
Razors	Gillette, Schick (Energizer)	Dollar Shave Club, Harry's, Ella
Contact lenses	J&J's Acuvue, Bausch & Lomb	Hubble Contacts
Shoes	Traditional shoes stores	Allbirds, Jack Erwin, M.Gemi
Grocery	Bricks and mortar grocery stores	Meal Kits
Pet food	Pet food retail stores	Ollie, The Farmer's Dog, NomNomNom
Mattresses	Sealy, Serta, Simmons, Tempur-Pedic	Casper, Helix Sleep, Loom & Leaf, Needle, Purple, Saatva, Tuft & Needle, Boll & Branch, Yogabed

Examples of upcoming DTC brands going after incumbents

Data is at the center of the DTC economy. It is the enabler, the competitive edge and the link between all systems, from production to fulfillment to customer service. The DTC economy will cover all imaginable categories of consumer products, from anti-aging products to cars to eyewear to food, footwear, sleepwear, pet care, vitamins, watches, sexual wellness and other sectors. Hundreds of startups and billions of VC and PE dollars will fuel the revolution, as technology drastically reduces the barriers to entry and cost for challenger brands. This poses a significant threat to incumbents and the largest, most recognized brands will be under attack by smaller, more nimble and well-financed companies, some of which don't even exist today. Companies such as P&G, J&J, Nestlé, Coca-Cola, PepsiCo, Snapple, L'Oréal, Estée Lauder, Kimberly-Clark, Tyson, General Mills, Nike, Adidas, ASICS, Gillette, Chanel, H&M, Tiffany & Co, LVMH, Colgate-Palmolive, Fruit of the Loom, Victoria's Secret, The Gap and Swatch Group are on notice.

Of course, these large brands are not going to sit on their hands. Some will build or continue to develop and improve their own DTC business. Some will acquire nimble pure DTC plays, while other will simply miss the boat. For example, Edgewell Personal Care, which owns brands like Schick (razors), Banana Boat (sunscreen) and Wet Ones (moist wipes), acquired Harry's in May 2019 for $1.4 billion, following Unilever's acquisition of Dollar Shave Club in July 2016 for a reported value of $1 billion and Procter & Gamble's acquisition of Walker & Company in December 2018.

Payment as part of the purchasing experience

The act of payment and product acquisition are not always in synch and don't necessarily happen at the same time. Sometimes we pay before we get the products, sometimes we pay simultaneously and other times we pay after. Here are a few examples:

TIMING OF PAYMENT	EXAMPLES
Before transaction	When I buy a ticket to go to Barcelona on Expedia, my credit card is charged before my trip, which can be months before I actually enjoy sitting on the plane.
During transaction	When I buy apples at my local farmer's market, I give $3.25 in cash to the merchant and he hands me the apples at the same time. The payment coincides with receiving the product.
After transaction	When I buy a property and I have a mortgage, I pay monthly at the same time I enjoy my new home. Sometimes, car dealerships offer some interest-free payments when the first payment is made three months after the car has been delivered. In a restaurant, I order the food, I consume it and at the very end, I pay. This happens after I enjoyed the food.

Payment timing examples

Like price, the mechanism by which money is exchanged for a product or services has to be substantiated in the Claim, as it can play a critical role in the decision to buy. For example, if you want to buy a property and the seller will only sell with a 20% down payment, if you can't afford that large down payment, then the Claim is not aligned with the Pain and you won't be able to acquire the property. No transaction takes place. However, the experience of the actual payment is part of the A3 alignment.

A quiet revolution is happening now: Reverse Movement

A movement is happening now in consumer commerce that is taking place from brands to consumers. I call it the *Reverse Movement,* where product offerings, ease and convenience are brought and delivered to the consumer, instead of the consumer having to look for, compare, evaluate and acquire products or services. Here are a few examples of that new phenomenon:

- When you buy a product in an Apple Store, you don't have to grab the product, find the cash register, stay patiently in line and then pay. The Apple Store associate gets the product for you and the cash register "comes" to you. They process your credit card transaction where you stand and then you simply walk out of the store with your newly acquired iPhone or Apple Watch. Your receipt is emailed to you.

- At JFK Airport, there is an area near the departure gate where travelers can plug in their devices and work. Without leaving their seat, travelers can order food and wine from a tablet.

- With Uber, the car comes to you wherever you are. You don't have to walk one or two blocks in New York in the cold and soggy snow in the hopes that when you raise your hand, a cab will pull over to get you to your destination. Uber delivers easy, convenient and ubiquitous access.

- Instacart now offers same-day grocery delivery including thousands of products. Fresh avocados, eggs and milk from Whole Foods are delivered to you within two hours. Other companies like DoorDash, Peapod, Postmates and Target (via its $550 million acquisition of Shipt) are offering similar grocery delivery services.

- Many trees are now saved because there is no need anymore for paper airline tickets or boarding passes. Flying to Detroit? No problem. You book it online and your boarding pass magically appears on your smartphone in a 2D scan code. In the old days, you had to go to a travel agency or the airport to get your ticket printed and then wait a long time in line at the airport to get your boarding pass printed. Thankfully, those days are long gone.

- Tele-medicine is happening. Doctors conduct visits via video calls with patients who are using devices from the comfort of their home. These devices can measure some vital signs that the doctor can access and interpret in real time. The acne treatment brand Curology is offering treatment online by connecting consumers with a medical professional to prescribe the right product.

- Buying a new Android phone? No need to go somewhere to make your purchase. Companies like Enjoy, described later in this chapter, will bring your phone to you, process the credit card and even set the phone up for you to make sure everything works and that your pictures on your old phone are transferred to the new one.

- Looking for a financial advisor? Fisher Investment will come to your place to meet, and then all the onboarding process is done by phone, email and on the Web.

- If you need dog sitting, Rover.com will send someone to pick up your dog and pet sit for a few days, then bring your beloved pet back to your home when you're back from the Bahamas!

- BabyQuip delivers a crib or stroller to your hotel or the airport when you travel. They rent safe, clean and good-quality baby equipment, saving you a lot of hassle when you travel with children. When you are ready to leave, they will pick up and dismantle the equipment, then take it away and clean it for the next family.

- No time to fill up your car with gas? Not a problem—Booster will do it while you work. Their slogan is "You park. We pump." They also will clean your windows, check your tire pressure and replace your wiper blades if necessary. Filld is offering a similar service, with the motto "Never stop for gas again."

All these examples are showing how various companies focus on the A3 alignment to vastly improve delivery of products and services. This is profound and demonstrates how Reverse Movement puts the customer at the center, with goods and services flowing to consumers, rather than the reverse.

ENJOY

An awesome delivery experience

In 2017, just a few days before Christmas, I bought a new iPhone for my wife since her iPhone 5 was starting to show some irreversible signs of aging. I ordered the new phone from my AT&T account and had the option of having it delivered for free the following day.

I realized that it was Saturday, so they would deliver the new phone on Sunday. Several delivery times were suggested to me. I chose 11 a.m.

Lo and behold, around 9 a.m. on Sunday, I received a text message from a person named Thomas. It read: "Hey Philippe, this is Thomas, your expert with Enjoy. I'll be delivering your new iPhone and helping you set it up! If you can confirm that today at 11 still works for you, we'll be all set!" I responded yes and two hours later, my doorbell rang, much to the excitement of my dog Rio, and Thomas, a young, energetic person, introduced himself.

He quickly set up the new iPhone, explained how to transfer the data from my wife's old iPhone and answered all the questions I had. He was nice, polite, knowledgeable and very clear. It was a very efficient process that took about 20 minutes. On his way out, he left my wife with a nice Enjoy grocery bag.

I would have never expected such an experience from AT&T, based on previous long wait times in their store and my numerous frustrating inter- actions calling their 800 number. I was originally thinking that I would have to drive to the AT&T store, wait in line for 30 minutes and have someone who does not quite know how to set up a new iPhone desper- ately try to help me.

As I talked with Thomas about Enjoy, he explained to me that they are not part of AT&T. No wonder I had a great experience! Based on my expe- rience and looking at the company website, Enjoy clearly understands that innovation is all about redefining the user experience. Their home page greets visitors with: "Welcome to a new kind of delivery experience." The subtitle is clear, concise and to the point: "Reimagine buying tech prod- ucts with free same-day delivery and setup by a friendly Expert." They indeed deliver and set up tech products with same-day delivery (as soon as 30 minutes after purchase), where and when you want it, and make sure it works for you. Best of all, it is totally free to the buyer.

Enjoy buys inventory, keeping it locally so that it is ready to be delivered quickly. They work with brands like AT&T, Google (for Android phones), Sonos (music products) and Magic Leap (virtual reality gear). They currently cover 51 cities. Every expert is an employee who receives over 160 hours of training. At the end of 2018, the company had more than 500 employees and had raised $80 million in venture capital, enjoying (pun intended) very fast growth. Their backers are among the best VC firms in the Valley: Kleiner Perkins, Oak Investment Partners and Andreessen Horowitz. Enjoy was founded in 2014 by Ron Johnson, who previously was the CEO of JCPenney and then ran the Apple Retail business. Apple stores are widely recognized as the world's most successful retail operation, with nearly 400 locations in 13 countries, boasting one of the highest revenues per square foot in the world.

MACY'S

Losing its third alignment

Some companies just can't maintain their alignment.

On November 13, 2018, *Mad Money* host Jim Cramer shared his view about Macy's and JCPenney becoming relics of the retail past. Are bricks and mortar becoming irrelevant during a time when Amazon Prime, one-click purchase, same-day delivery, peer reviews, recommendations, social media shopping and mobile shopping are embraced by more and more people?

Sales at Macy's have been declining over the past four years. They peaked at $28.1 billion in FY2014 (Macy's FY ends January 31) and closed at $24.8 billion in FY2017. During the same period, Amazon grew revenue from $89 billion to $177.9 billion (Amazon's fiscal year ends on December 31) at an annual growth of 26%.

In order to compare the top-line growth rates of both companies, I normalized revenues using 2009 revenue, because it is the year when both companies had the same revenue ($24 billion), and plotted the revenue change up to 2017. Here's how that looks:

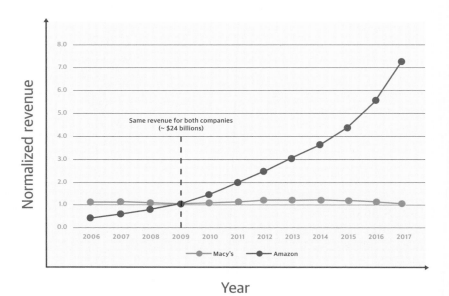

Normalized revenue of Macy's versus Amazon from 2006 to 2017

Now, let's examine the evolution of the value of the stock. Just looking at the graph, it is not hard to decide which stock to invest in. Let's do the math on how revenue growth correlates with shareholder value creation. If you had bought $100 of Macy's stock on the last trading day of 2009 and the same $100 of Amazon's stock exactly eight years later, your Macy's stock would be worth $150.30, and your Amazon position would be worth $869.37. So, while you would have made 1.5 times your money in Macy's, you would have made close to nine times your money in Amazon.

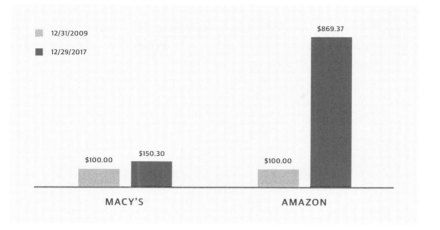

$869.37

$150.30

$100.00 $100.00

MACY'S   AMAZON

Stock value appreciation of Macy's versus Amazon from 2009 to 2017

As expected, the stock appreciation is well correlated with the revenue growth. The market greatly rewards companies with the fastest revenue growth rates. This also illustrates the fact that anemic growth leads to irrelevancy (no investors are excited to invest) and eventually death.

Here is Jim Cramer's view on Macy's defense argument for its poor performance: "Instead, we heard the same kind of tale of woe, the struggling stories, the same defensive nature, with the only twist being a better control of inventory and a sense that they can continue to plod along."

It is very hard for Macy's to compete with the same kind of consumer experience Amazon offers. For Macy's, there is simply too much distance that separates the store and the shopper's attributes. If I walk into a Macy's store, Macy's does not know my tastes, what I bought in the past and if I liked or disliked a previously purchased product. They don't know how much time I spend in the store, what aisle I visit, what products I take off the shelf to look at or my credit card number. They don't know the zip code I live in, which is a good proxy for how much money I make. Amazon magically knows all that information.

It is not trivial to grow revenue in a mature market that is not growing as fast. In fact, the most effective way is to seize market share from a competitor. It is unclear who these competitors would be in the case of Macy's. On the other hand, US retail eCommerce grew at a compound annual growth rate of 11.9% per year between 2012 and 2016, grabbing only 7.2% of the US retail market in 2015. So, it is easy to extrapolate and see how much growth potential eCommerce has to offer over the next ten years.

It is hard to find a solid reason and a convincing, defensible argument for keeping these old brick-and-mortar retail businesses alive. In a way, it is not too dissimilar from imagining the death of the taxi industry once safe and autonomous cars start picking you up to take you to perhaps the last Macy's store on earth. Remember when we used to go to Blockbuster to grab a DVD movie for a nice Saturday night with the family? Feels like ancient history.

SELLING TO
THE FEDERAL GOVERNMENT

A difficult A3 alignment to realize

The federal government does not buy like any other businesses. It does not live in the private commercial world. Small businesses sell about $100 billion of services and goods to the US federal government each year. So, if you are a small business and want a piece of that pie, how do you go about getting it?

The process is inherently complicated and intimidating.

First off, the business owner has to find its NAICS (North American Industry Classification System) code and the Federal Supply Classification (FSC) code for his or her business. The business needs to be certified and registered as a GC (government contractor) in order to receive a DUNS number (Data Universal Numbering System, which is managed by Dun & Bradstreet) and be in the SAM (System for Award Management) database. The business also must verify that it is indeed a small business by determining if it qualifies for 8(a), SDB or HUBZone certification.

By checking the FedBizOpps website, the company can see what procurement opportunities are available and check current open bids. Federal acquisitions are legally regulated by the Federal Acquisition Regulations (FAR) and the Defense Federal Acquisition Regulation Supplement (DFARS). Each federal agency produces an Annual Procurement Forecast as required by the Small Business Act. This gives a sense of the types of products and services procured by the federal government.

Then, the small business has to sign a "contract vehicle" with the government. It basically pre-authorizes the business to sell to the government and become an approved supplier. Getting on the GSA (General Services Administration) Schedule can be a tedious process and can take months. An easier approach, often used, is to simply become a subcontractor or an entity that already has a contract vehicle in place.

After that, local Procurement Center Representatives (PCRs) provide tips and offer training to navigate the atrocious waters of working with the government and finding the right party who might be interested in your products or services. Other services are offered by the Office of Government Contracting and Business Development (GC/BD), which is part of the Small Business Administration (SBA). Part of their job is to make sure that the federal government purchases at least 23% from small businesses as mandated by the Small Business Act of 1953.

Then the real fun starts: finding out who might be interested in your offering and where they are located. Although all the information is publicly available, finding the right opportunity and fit is a tall order in the vast jungle of the federal government. The internet is a great place to start, but there are also industry or sector events and support groups to help. Finally, all bids are broadcast and made available publicly. The winner, hopefully your business, is then rewarded with the GSA contract. As described on the GSA.gov website, "As the acquisition arm of the federal government, GSA plays a vital role in connecting the private sector with federal agencies fulfilling their business needs." GSA uses various types of contracts, but the primary one is called the GSA Schedules, or Multiple Award Schedules.

The paradox of selling to the federal government is that it is a convoluted, tedious and complicated process with a large number of rigid rules.

That's the difficult part. The good news, though, is that all the information on how to navigate these waters and what the government is looking for is widely available and published for all to see. It invites fair competition and offers a chance for any small business—regardless of its size, location, who runs it or any other subjective considerations—to win the business.

This entire process is a good illustration of the A3 alignment axis. The federal government buys goods and services a certain way. Just going to Washington and knocking on the right doors simply won't work. Small businesses must comply with rules and regulations and accept the fact that the process moves at its own governmental speed, under its own convoluted process. Otherwise, no transaction can be completed.

CASE STUDY

WHAT WE HAVE LEARNED

➤ The third axis of alignment is Purchase ⟷ Sale.

➤ Once the prospect is convinced that the claim will solve his/her pain at an acceptable price and terms, then the next step in the process is to acquire the product or service.

➤ The way a prospect wants to acquire and the way the product is sold in the marketplace have to be aligned for a transaction to take place.

➤ The appropriate go-to-market strategy must be carefully crafted, as there are many ways to sell a product such as direct, retail, via value-added reseller, licensing and OEM, etc.

➤ More attention has been given to this third axis of alignment recently. It's the beginning of a quiet revolution I call The Reverse Movement. It is a profound change with lasting effects, where products and services and ease-of-transaction are delivered to the customer, not the opposite as it has been up until now.

➤ Misalignment between purchase and sale decreases the opportunity for a transaction and therefore negatively affects revenue growth.

CASE STUDIES

➤ Enjoy: An awesome delivery experience

➤ Macy's: Losing its third alignment

NEXT CHAPTER

➤ Focuses on A4, the fourth axis of alignment: Delight versus Offering.

"

Disappointment is a sort of bankruptcy—
the bankruptcy of a soul that expends too much
in hope and expectation.

ERIC HOFFER
author and philosopher

FOURTH AXIS

Delight versus Offering

ALIGNMENT AXES	CUSTOMER		BUSINESS	GOAL
1	Pain	→ | ←	Claim	Real painkiller
2	Perception	→ | ←	Message	Compelling story
3	Purchase	→ | ←	Sale	Frictionless transaction
4	Delight	→ | ←	Offering	Insane delight

The fourth axis of alignment in the *A4 Precision Alignment*™ methodology is between the delight the customer is expecting after the acquisition of the product and the experience he or she receives using the product. This story helps illustrate the concept.

McDonald's or l'Assiette Champenoise?

In France, there is a little village called Tinqueux in the northeastern part of the country, in the Marne region. It sits very close to the southwest side of Reims, known for its Roman Catholic church, its bloody battle of the Marne in 1944–45 and above all, its enviable position as the Champagne capital. This is where Veuve Clicquot-Ponsardin, Taittinger and Pommery established their roots in the middle of the 18th century.

There is a special place that is not to be missed in Tinqueux. It's a restaurant called l'Assiette Champenoise. Its kitchen is run by Chef Arnaud Lallement, who received his first star from the Michelin Guide at the age of 26 and currently boasts three stars. I have to confess that I have never set foot in l'Assiette Champenoise, but just reading its French menu uncontrollably triggered the Pavlov reflex and by closing my eyes, I could imagine dining there with the people I cherish the most in my life.

One winter day, I was meeting a client in Denver. My flight was late, and it was very cold and windy. I was kicking myself for not having brought my gloves and I was starving. The salted peanuts served on my delayed Southwest flight did not really fill my stomach. Reluctantly, I pushed open the door of a downtown McDonald's and ordered a Big Mac accompanied by French fries. I paid $3.99 plus tax and, ten minutes later, I was content that I was no longer hungry but promised myself that this was my last experience at McDonald's. I have to confess, I am not a fan of fast food both because of the taste and how unhealthy it is. This was back in 2008; I kept my promise and have not been in a McDonald's since that cold evening in Colorado.

No offense to McDonald's. It is an amazing global company. It generated over $22.8 billion in sales in 2017 and has one of the most recognized brands in the world. It delights kids, mothers and fathers and grandparents alike. It offers a great deal of convenience by being fast and affordable.

So, I wondered, after someone has eaten à l'Assiette Champenoise or McDonald's and is leaving the place, what's the difference? Apart from having a much lighter wallet after leaving l'Assiette Champenoise, I would argue that there's not much difference. In the end, it's the same thing: one has filled one's stomach with food and satisfied one of the most basic functions of life: eating and drinking in order to live another day.

However, there is a fundamental difference when that person walks into both places. It has to do with the fourth axis of alignment: it's all about expectation. That really makes all the difference. If a person walks into a McDonald's, the expectation is that there will be a line, it may not have the most tantalizing aroma, the music may not fit with the person's tastes, and of course, the food might not be the healthiest meal. But it is fast and cheap. Now, if the same person passes through the elegant doors of l'Assiette Champenoise, then the expectation in terms of quality, from the greeting at the door to the unobtrusive but amazingly efficient and personalized service, the high quality of the food, the pleasant visual experience, the subtle balance between the wine and the food and the memory it will imprint for many years to come, makes all the difference.

In the end, both l'Assiette Champenoise and McDonald's are very successful businesses. While very similar and at the same time very different on many levels, their success is due to a solid alignment between what is expected, which is radically different in both cases, and what is delivered.

There is only ONE business on this planet

What is the difference between Caterpillar, Farmers Insurance Group, Ford Motor Company, Krispy Kreme and Pixar Animation Studios? The answer might shock you: at a fundamental level, there is none. All these five companies are in the exact same business with the exact same goal and purpose:

MANUFACTURE
and
DELIVER
DELIGHT

The one and only business on the planet

Let me say it again, as this is really important: any company or enterprise, small or large, anywhere in the world, selling to consumers or other businesses or the government, regardless of the pain it addresses, is in the same business: to manufacture and deliver delight. In other words, there is only one unique business in the world: the manufacture and delivery of delight.

This is a matter of survival. Without it, decline into irrelevancy and death is almost certain as a competitor swoops in and delivers the expected delight. Here are a few examples:

- One of the best examples of customer delight and loyalty is Harley-Davidson. When Harley believed they were selling motorcycles, they almost went out of business. When they realized they were selling permission for middle-aged accountants to dress in leather and let their bad-boy flags fly as they drove through small towns, the business took off. Their fans are so loyal that people tattoo the company logo on their bodies. That's when you know you've delighted... when the ink goes on!

- McDonald's was started in 1940 by Richard and Maurice McDonald and today boasts about 37,000 locations around the world, delighting 69 million customers every day, young and old, with their hamburgers, French fries, salads and milkshakes served in 100 countries in cities from Beijing to Milan to Seattle.

- Farmers Insurance has been delivering delight since 1928 and currently serves more than 10 million households with 19 million individual policies across the United States.

- Pixar, a subsidiary of Walt Disney Studios, continues to delight children and adults, inspiring them to dream. Their films elicit emotions, speak to our hearts and make us smile, laugh and cry. During the weekend of June 16, 2018, Pixar generated a record-setting $180 million at the domestic box office with the release of *Incredibles 2*. This was the highest-ever box office sales for an animated film, delighting about 20 million kids and adults over a 48-hour period.

- Ford made 6.6 million people happy around the world in 2017, when they delivered brand-new shiny Fiesta, Focus, Fusion and Taurus cars and of course, the iconic Mustang.

If some level of delight were not met, all these companies would have been long gone. You may like them or not, but their customer delight is what makes them iconic and pillars of American industry.

In the end, what the company does is not that relevant. What makes a company great is the level of delight they truly deliver to their customers. This is the only real measure of success. The amount of delight translates into word-of-mouth, growth, profitability and the sustained creation of shareholder value.

At the end of the day, every business, whether small or large, mom-and-pop or multinational corporation, from New York to Shanghai, is in the same business. It's all about the obsessive pursuit of delight, satisfaction and happiness. Delight is to business growth what oxygen is to every human being.

Is it really "delight"?

During a breakfast meeting in the fall of 2018 at Buck's, the iconic Silicon Valley restaurant, Geoffrey Moore shared an interesting observation with me. He explained that the notion of delight and, more recently, *customer success management* really happened in the 20th century. It became relevant and important because supplies of goods and services became abundant, opening doors for a high level of competition. During the previous century, supply was low, demand was high, and therefore people could put up with mediocre products and bad experiences. Access was important, not delight.

I have been challenged about the choice of the word *delight*. It's a point well taken. For example, when a patient takes drugs to fight cancer, it would indeed be inappropriate to talk about delight. Businesses selling to other businesses (B2B) are sometimes "delight enablers." Their customers may be buying their products to delight their own customers (typically consumers). In some cases, the main driver for B2B transactions might be more about greed or fear and less about delight.

What delight do you deliver when you sell plastic pipes to transport sewer water? Ask Walter Wang, the company president and CEO of JM Eagle, the world's largest provider of plastic polyvinyl chloride (PVC) and polyethylene (PE) pipes. The employees truly take pride in what they do. Wang stated it well:

 We are really proud of what we do.
A very simple manufacturing business,
but we do believe our product brings
the essence of life.

JM Eagle produces 2.2 billion pounds of pipe every year, shipping anywhere across the globe. Their products are the foundation of our underground infrastructure for water, gas and electricity. They are there, below our feet. We don't see them; we don't think about them. Yet, without them, our lives would be miserable. Their products last 100 to 150 years.

The company's mission statement reflects their commitment to delight their customers, wherever they are:

We at JM Eagle think of ourselves as a different kind of company, doing our part to make the world a better place. This pursuit is realized through an unwavering commitment to leadership in everything we do.

We don't just see to the needs of our customers, we also strive endlessly to surpass them. We don't just produce excellent products, we also work for continuous improvement. We don't just talk about quality, we also endorse a quality management system, maintain ISO certification in our plants, and ensure our pipe meets or exceeds the most stringent quality standards.

And we do this all with respect for the beauty and fragility of the world and the well-being of its inhabitants, ensuring that our business makes a positive contribution to the environment, the communities we serve, our customers, and our employees.

How inspiring! **No matter the business, delight has to be the endgame.** It drives commitment and sets a tangible, measurable goal. It puts the bar at a higher level. It makes people who are working hard proud of what they do. It gives them a purpose. It makes the world a better place. Happiness is not enough. Delight is what it's all about.

Intuit, the software company behind the popular TurboTax product and other personal finance management products, has a council that is driven by their *Design for Delight* motto. They have a lab called D2D (Design to Delight) to design with a purpose. When Scott Cook started Intuit back in 1983, there were no fewer than 46 companies offering software to help people manage their finances. Cook jokes that Intuit had the "47th mover advantage." While the first Intuit product only had one-third of the features the others offered, it had one major difference: it looked like a check register and individual checks, not like a spreadsheet. It was intuitive and easy to use. That was a turning point on the path to the amazing success of Cook's company.

By comparison, there is probably no more extreme example of A4 misalignment than Theranos, the company founded by Stanford drop-out Elizabeth Holmes on the promise of being able to perform hundreds of blood tests off a single drop of blood. This claim naturally triggered a high level of excitement, with the potential to eliminate painful blood draws. But not only was the premise medically unsound and the prom-ises unfounded, the company leaders falsified results, putting patients at risk. Holmes and her second in command lied to partners, investors and regulators over a period of years, and now face a battery of fraud charges.

The question is: how much delight?

The answer is simple, but not easy: the amount of delight delivered has to be slightly above what is expected from customers. The challenge is: what exactly is that expectation? How much does it change from one customer to the next? And who sets it?

I came to believe that the promise of delight is overrated, and the management of expectation is underrated. This equation needs to be rebalanced.

The expectation has to be clearly defined, articulated and communi-cated by the company to its prospects. As I covered in Chapter 5, this is what the A2 alignment is all about and why it is so important. No one else should alter the expression of the claim. It is the defining force behind the notion of expectation setting. The press, prospects, a disgruntled employee, a lost customer, board members, partners or investors should not be allowed to set or change the customer's expectation. They must be the echo chamber, the amplifier, the channel to carry that voice, but in no circumstances should they attempt to define, tweak or change it. This is like the conductor of a symphony orchestra: he conducts the music based on a set score and he cannot change any of the notes or dynamics written in the score. Otherwise, music could not perpetuate and be true to the creativity of the composer. Imagine if a conductor changes the Bruch Violin Concerto No. 1 in G minor. Bruch's idea, when he composed the masterpiece in 1866, would be altered, and who knows what it would have become over time through even the smallest changes. The integrity of the artist's voice and creativity would not be preserved. Paradoxically, within that fundamental constraint, the conductor still has a large degree of freedom to express the piece in his own terms. He has some latitude and some level of freedom on the tempo, and on volume balance among the various groups of instruments. He has a reasonable amount of leeway for the dynamic and to extract the best from each musician in a cohesive way that truly delivers magic, or delight I should say!

The impedance mismatch of delight

In mid 2018, I came across an article that was published in *Fortune,* an interview with Byron Deeter, a partner at the VC firm Bessemer Venture Partners. Deeter joined Bessemer in 2005 and is one of the most prosperous investors in SaaS and Cloud, having led investments in highly successful publicly traded companies such as Box, Criteo, DocuSign, Twilio and promising private companies such as Gainsight, Intacct, SendGrid and Tile.

Bessemer is known for publishing their "anti-portfolio" page that lists companies the partners looked at and passed on but wished they had invested in. Most notably on Deeter's list are companies like Atlassian and Tesla. He test-drove the Tesla roadster back in 2006 and believed that the negative gross margins would not yield to a sustainable company. The Bessemer list includes marquee logos such as Airbnb, Apple, eBay, Facebook, FedEx, Google, Intel, Intuit, Kayak, PayPal and Snap.

When asked about the best business advice he'd ever received as an early founder, Deeter responded with a simple equation:

$$Success = Results - Expectations$$

Results are hard, but expectation management is often one of the most overlooked and underrated aspects of managing a business.

I could not agree more about the wisdom of Deeter's advice. A great expression of that notion is precisely what I define in the fourth axis of alignment in our *A4 Precision Alignment™* approach, where delivered delight has to be above the expectation and anticipation of that delight. Note that this can be achieved either by upping delight or by lowering expectations.

The amount of delight has to be slightly above expectations. If it is below, the misalignment generates a negative impact on the business and revenue growth will be adversely affected. Eventually revenue will start to erode. If it's too much above, then money is left on the table and pricing is not optimized, because customers would be willing to pay slightly more for the level of delight they actually experience.

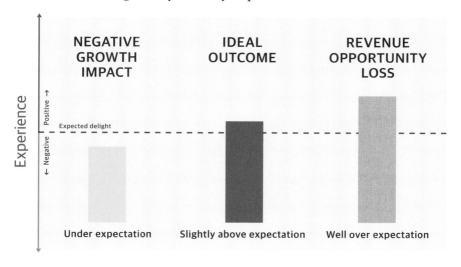

Again, the critical aspect is that the expected delight must be set by the company and should always remain under its total control.

So, I would propose a new equation for the A4 alignment:

Growth Contribution = Experienced Delight − Expected Delight

The invisible magic of delight

There are some products or services that delight us every day. We just don't pay attention to them. They are there, they are real and only the removal of them would unearth a sharp pain. I call that the *Invisible Magic of Delight*.
Here are a few examples of what I mean:

- When you open a faucet in your bathroom, the water magically flows. You expect it and can't imagine turning the faucet and not having the water pour out. What it takes to capture, redirect, treat, monitor and deliver water to each home's bathrooms, laundry room, kitchen and sprinkler system is quite remarkable. This is no small feat. Sometimes, we have to deal with losing water for a few hours during home or infrastructure construction. It takes only that first muscle-memory turn of the faucet, with no water coming out, to understand the magic of getting water anytime, all the time.

- When you sit on an airplane that rolls down the runway at a speed of 170 miles per hour, then takes off and magically floats, the complex machinery works. The Boeing Jumbo Jet 747, one of aviation's greatest achievements, was built at Boeing's Everett factory near Seattle. It was made of no fewer than 6 million parts and 250 kilometers of cables (if they were put in one straight line). It continues to fly today and is one of the most reliable planes ever built. It miraculously and consistently works, decade after decade.

- When you walk to a bank teller in Honolulu to withdraw $60, the machine magically gives you the banknotes. It takes 20 seconds. It works despite the complex global financial processes and security behind each single transaction.

- When you sit at your desk to call a customer on another continent 3,000 miles away, the dial tone is there, you hear the rings and the other person picks up and says, "Hello, John!" It works because of the very complex global telecom infrastructure across the world, with signals bouncing off geostationary satellites 22,236 miles above our heads or at a submarine depth equivalent to Everest on the floor of the largest oceans on the planet. The diameter of deepwater cables is about the size of a Magic Marker. It's truly magic.

- When you have mild muscle pain because you exercised a little too much yesterday, you take a couple pills of the nonsteroidal anti-inflammatory drug ibuprofen. Sure enough, after 30 minutes, you already feel better. It's magic, it's transparent, it's invisible and above all, it simply works!

It's when the taken-for-granted expectation is not met that delight, or the lack thereof, manifests itself. It's painful and it can be life threatening. The truly amazing thing about the examples above lies in the notion of hiding the complexity. It is hard to comprehend how these things work. For example, it is a challenge to understand the complexity of the technology running inside a smartphone. It's a world of small and delicate wires, batteries, printed circuit boards, controllers, loudspeakers, microphones, sensors, semiconductors, antennas, connectors, plastic parts and bezels and of course, the most visible component of all: the screen. When it doesn't work, frustration flares up and a strong sense of betrayal is felt. How can my phone let me down?!

Delight is delivered to us every second of our lives. It is magic; it is transparent and enchanting. We just don't always realize it until it no longer is.

The new freedom of expression

For a long time, consumers and businesses exercised their freedom of choice: if they did not like a product or had a bad experience, they would vote with their wallet and buy a competitive product. Had a bad experience with BMW? Next car will be a Lexus. Struggling with customer support from Comcast's supposedly high-speed internet services? I'll switch to AT&T. The problem is that employees of companies providing products or services that were not aligned with customers' expectations had little incentive to change the way that business was run. While they pretended to care, they knew that losing you as a customer wouldn't make any significant difference to their business. The customer service representatives or their boss wouldn't lose their job over your defection.

But now, things are different. Voices are amplified, thanks to social networks.

Social networks such as Facebook, Instagram, Twitter, YouTube and other platforms give anyone a voice that can be amplified instantaneously at a massive scale and shared with millions of users. The discontent of users can now be expressed in a few clicks and within a few seconds is reverberating via sharing, likes, re-tweeting and commenting, making its way all the way to the CEO.

Here is an example of freedom of expression and delight gone off the rails.

In December 2008, Canadian country-and-western singer Dave Carroll had his $3,500 Taylor acoustic guitar severely damaged by United Airline baggage handlers at Chicago's O'Hare International Airport. Frustrated by the bad handling of the case and the poor reaction from the airline, Carroll decided to write three songs, appropriately called "United Breaks Guitars." Released in July 2009, the trio became a hit on iTunes and YouTube and most definitely caught the attention of the airline. The original spark for writing the songs came when Carroll asked himself, "If Michael Moore were a singer-songwriter, what would he do?" Viewership of the video jumped to 150,000 views the following day, half a million views days later, and had reached 18 million in 2018.

This was a public humiliation for United. It failed to appropriately and publicly repair the damage it had caused. The situation could have been handled correctly (pun intended!) from the beginning, turning the disaster into a positive outcome for United.

In May of 2012, Carroll decided to write a book that he cleverly entitled *United Breaks Guitars: The Power of One Voice in the Age of Social Media,* where he shared his experience.

Clearly, United did not put customers and passengers at the center of its business. The lack of compassion, basic understanding and ability to deal with difficult situations created a huge PR headache for the company and cost United a significant amount of money.

It would have cost United $1,200 to fix the Carroll situation (and the guitar). Journalist Chris Ayres of *The Times* Online in the UK wrote, "Within four days of the song going online, the gathering thunderclouds of bad PR caused United Airlines' stock price to suffer a mid-flight stall, and it plunged by 10 percent, costing shareholders $180 million. Which, incidentally, would have bought Carroll more than 51,000 replacement guitars."

One would think that United would have learned from the Carroll incident, but no. In another major mishap, in April 2017, a doctor was forcefully removed from a United flight in order to make room for crew members, as if they are more important than customers! A flurry of comments along the lines of "and now United breaks passengers" was added to Carroll's videos. Southwest jumped on the opportunity to issue a statement saying, "We beat our competitors, not our passengers!"

What a lesson! The impact of losing customers can be dramatic, as I will illustrate below.

The sinking towers

Anyone following San Francisco real estate is familiar with the saga of the Millennium Tower. The tallest residential building in the city, construction on the tower took four years. The penthouse alone sold for more than $9 million. Six years later, the building had sunk more than a foot and was tilting two inches. There are numerous lawsuits pending and no one knows how this matter will ultimately be resolved.

Sinking tower? Not a great thing to happen.

In physics, we have the law of conservation of energy. In business, a similar law exists: the number of customers always conserves. That means that the total number of customers a company had last year is equal to the sum of customers that stayed this year plus the number of lost customers. On top of that, new customers are added. This law of conservation does not apply for bookings or revenue, because the money paid by a given customer can change from one year to the next, if the price is changed or if a customer buys less of a product. In fact, beyond calculating averages, there is no obvious correlation between the number of customers and the transacted dollar value of these customers. For example, a business can lose customers but increase revenue from the previous customers who are buying more.

"Inspired" by the sinking Millennium Tower, I created a tool to visualize this effect. Here is how it works: Each year the number of customers is represented by a bar graph. It is color coded, so the top of the bar is in blue and represents the number of new customers acquired during the year. Just below, in green, is the number of customers who became new customers last year, then in gray, the ones who became customers two years or more ago. In orange, below the baseline, are all the customers lost during the current year. This is the sunk part of the column or the "tower."

If you take the "visible" part of the tower (above the ground level) from last year, then it needs to be the exact same size as next year's tower, including the sunk part, but excluding new customers (which, again, are added on top in blue). In other words, the number of customers from last year has to remain the exact same number of customers who stayed this year plus the number of customers lost this year.

Here is a graph that illustrates an example of the concept.

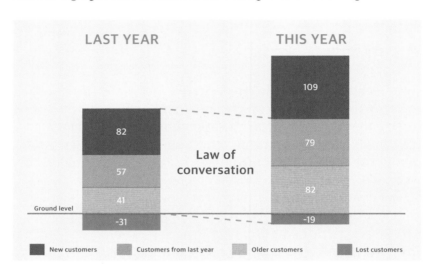

Conservation of number of customers

In this example, last year, the company added 82 new customers and had 57 that were added the year before, plus 41 older customers. So, the total of active customers last year was 82 + 57 + 41 = 180. Now this year, each customer either remained active or was lost. If you take the 82 new customers acquired last year, 79 remained active, which means the company lost two customers. They are part of the 19 lost customers. Now, if you add the customers from last year, the customers from the previous years and the lost customers, you get 79 + 82 + 19 = 180. This is how the number of customers conserves from one year to the next.

I call this approach the *Sinking Tower* model. The idea came from one of our Blue Dots clients who had an average top-line growth of 16% and wanted to increase its growth rate by 25%, i.e. reach a growth of 20%. We did our Sinking Tower analysis based on the data for the past six years, and here is what the company's graph looked like:

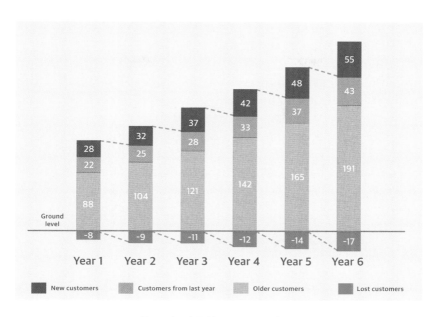

Example of Sinking Tower analysis

We realized that this particular client was building a tower on quicksand. So, while he kept adding floors on the top of the tower (the blue part), the entire tower, like the Millennium Tower in San Francisco, was actually sinking. Customer churn caused the sinking. If our client had stopped construction (i.e. did not add any new customers during the six-year period), the tower would sink at a rate of 5% per year. However, because the company was very good at adding new customers, much faster than the ones who churned, the top of the tower was growing at a rate of 16%. By cutting the churn rate in half, the top line could now grow at 17.1% without hiring one additional salesperson, up from 15.6% with the previous churn. We also did the analysis as if the company had zero churn. In that scenario, the top line would have grown at an average of 18.7%. Of course, this is a theoretical case, as it is very hard to have no churn.

So, by cutting the churn in half, the company would increase its topline growth by 10%. Here is another way to look at it: at the same churn rate, in order to have the same top-line growth, the company would need to increase its new customer acquisition rate by 25%. In other words, instead of adding a total of 267 new customers over the six years, the company would have to add 334 customers, i.e. 67 more customers over the same period of time, instead of convincing 38 existing customers to not defect. This is a much taller order.

Our client was losing too many customers from one year to the next. Digging deeper, what we found was interesting. It looked like most of the customers they were losing had been with them for six quarters. It turned out that every 1.5 years, the company had increased its pricing, which contributed to losing the most price-sensitive customers. We advised the company to manage its pricing differently and to over-communicate to existing customers, far in advance, the justification for the new pricing, which resulted in 21% of their growth rate the following year.

How churn affects revenue growth

Lowering the level of churn can have a dramatic effect on top-line growth. Here is an example for a company growing at 10% per year. If you analyze the top-line growth rate over six years and measure the average top-line growth rate for the last three years as a function of various annual churn rates, here is what the analysis reveals:

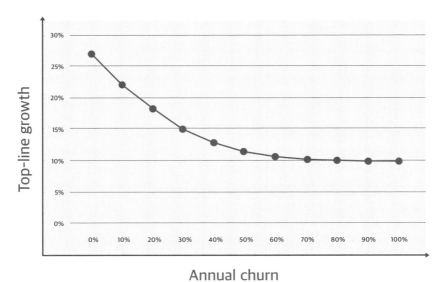

Sensitivity analysis

Of course, if the churn is very high, the growth rate is limited to the inorganic growth of the company, i.e. by just adding new customers, which is 10% in our example. If the company wants to double its growth rate to 20%, the graph above shows that the churn would have to be no more than 15%. If, on the other extreme, there was no churn at all, the top line would grow at an average of 27% per year, which is almost three times the growth rate generated by adding new customers alone. Note that this analysis assumes no price increase over the years.

This analysis applies to companies that either have a consumable product or a recurring revenue model. When it comes to durable products or services that are expected to last, then the aspect of NPS (Net Promoter Score) becomes critical for growth, because customers work as promoters (hopefully not detractors) rather than repeat purchasers. For instance, my GE Monarch appliances failed faster than I anticipated. Not only did I switch when I had to replace them sooner than expected, but I advised others not to buy the brand. On the other hand, I love my Miele dishwasher, and while I'm not going to buy another one next year, I am vocal in my enthusiasm.

This illustrates the power of subscription-based business models and why they are rewarded a much higher valuation than one-off business models. They drive a high growth rate, and by keeping a low churn rate, they are a lot less dependent on adding new customers, which is expensive. This is why companies such as Netflix, cellular phone companies and internet service providers have done so well.

The Engagement Triangle

I wanted to develop a tool that visually demonstrates the level of customer engagement over time, with strong signals when customers churn. As the model above illustrates, any business that generates revenue through a subscription model is greatly impacted every time they lose a customer for two main reasons:

1. They have already spent the money on marketing, convincing that prospect to buy, and then delivering the product and onboarding the customer. The marketing, sales and onboarding costs are sunk costs, so the impact of losing that customer on net profit is important, because the lifetime value (LTV) is decreased.

2. If customers leave because they are not happy, then it is important to understand where the frustration comes from, because it is negatively impacting future growth.

Where did the A4 misalignment between the expected and received delight happen? What was the cause? How did it materialize? Are there early-warning indicators that could have been put in place to avoid the situation? Can other current customers be affected? Is the business at risk of losing them too? If the customer left for reasons that have nothing to do with his/her experience with the product or service, then that's important to know as well.

The tool I created is a way to track how loyal each customer is over time, by visually plotting their engagement level and observing the velocity at which new customers are added and existing customers lost. This important tool displays the health of any kinds of recurring business models. It can be used in a variety of businesses. Here are some examples of recurring revenue:

- Netflix is charging $7.99 per month for its basic single-screen plan.

- Verizon is charging a family plan of $59.00 each month for wireless phones.

- CNN is charging a monthly fee of $6.95 for its Newswatch service.

- Chipotle tracks how frequently a family eats at any of their 2,000 locations around the world.

- Microsoft is charging $99.99 a year for its Office 365 home edition.

- And of course, any B2B subscription-based SaaS business.

It can also be applied to situations that are not monetary, such as, if American Airlines wants to track how many miles each of its customers flies or Jiffy Lube wants to know how many times per year its customers get an oil change.

In these businesses, what is important is the frequency of transactions and the average amount of money spent each time. The tool is called the *Engagement Triangle* because it displays the engagement level between every single customer and the business with a high degree of granularity.

Here is how it works. There is a horizontal and a vertical axis, each representing time. The horizontal axis tracks when the customer bought for the very first time and the vertical axis tracks time passing by. The unit of time, depending on the business, can be weeks, months, quarters or years. Each customer is represented by a horizontal line that progresses as long as the customer continues to be a customer. If during the period of time the customers stops being a customer (churns), then the line stops and turns red; otherwise, it continues until the end and remains blue.

Here is an example of two customers followed over a period of eight years. The blue customer became a customer during Year 3 and continues to be a customer at the end of Year 8. The red customer became a customer during Year 5 but stopped being a customer during Year 7, which is why the line turns red.

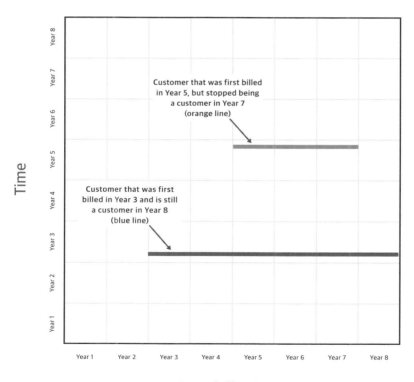

Start billing year

Examples of two customers in the Engagement Triangle

Now, let's take the example of a company that added 40 new customers in Year 1 and is growing at 10% a year, therefore ends Year 8 with a total of 454 customers. If the company had no churn, here is how the perfect Engagement Triangle would look:

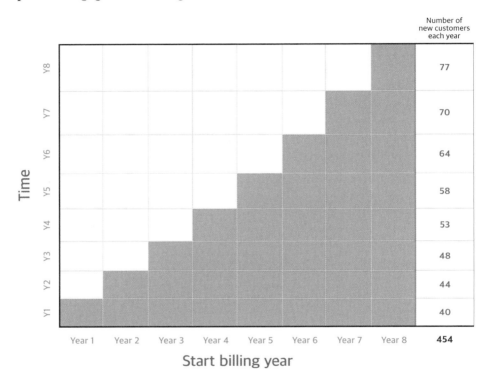

Perfect Engagement Triangle for a company with no churn

The triangle has a total of 454 lines, each representing a customer. There is no red bar since no customers churned. All the bars are blue because no customers defected. It is interesting to notice that the height of each year is increasing since the company is adding more and more new customers each year (in this case at an increased rate of 10% per year), which is a good indication of growth. Each horizontal band represents the cohort of all the new customers added that particular year.

Finally, one understands why it is always a triangle: a line cannot exist before a customer becomes a customer. This is why each single line can only start below the hypotenuse of the right triangle.

Of course, in real life, our company is not perfect and indeed some customers defected. Here is how the real Engagement Triangle looks:

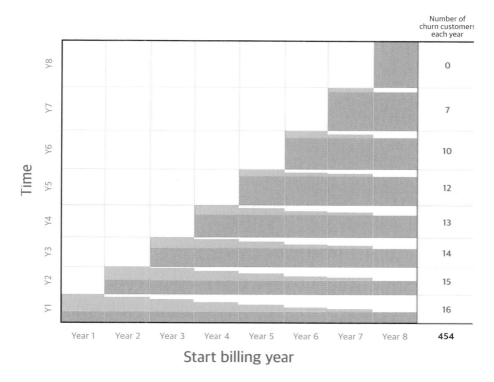

Examples of a real Engagement Triangle

The company lost 87 customers in total, or 19.2% during the eight-year period. Not surprisingly, no customers were lost in Year 8 since none of these new customers have been through the first annual renewal cycle yet. Conversely, the older the customers, the higher the churn, which makes sense.

Now, let's look at the impact of churn on revenue. If no customer had ever left, we could precisely measure the revenue that the company missed over time by prolonging each red line until Year 8. In our example above, if one assumes the company sells a subscription to businesses for $10,000 per month, the calculation shows that with no churn, the company would have revenues of $21.9 million, but because of churn, the missed revenue opportunity is $2.6 million, which represents 13% of realized revenue.

The model can be visually improved by adding another dimension. The idea is to color-code each bar based on the average amount paid by the customer each year. In most businesses, the goal is to generate more and more revenue per account over time. There are three cases where that can happen:

- **PRICE INCREASE.** The business increases its price to at least stay on par with inflation or indices such as the Consumer Price Index. This is sometimes called COLA, for Cost of Living Adjustment.

- **UPGRADE.** The customer upgrades. For example, I upgrade my Netflix subscription to the two-screen HD plan at $10.99 instead of one screen in Standard Definition at $7.99.

- **VOLUME INCREASE.** The customer buys more capacity. For example, I add a mobile phone line for my kids or buy more Salesforce.com CRM seats for my business because I am increasing the size of my sales team.

Here is an example of how to color-code each bar (representing each customer) using three colors (gray, blue and green). Imagine a business that sells cyber-security subscriptions to large corporations at an average price of $100,000 per year. If a customer spends less than $100,000, the bar is gray; if it spends between $100,001 and $500,000, it is blue; and if it spends more than $500,000, then the bar is green. In theory, the business will want to see each bar going from gray to blue to green. This is because the customer might be starting with a department or at a small scale and then if satisfied, will expand to other departments or other geographies, buying more and more. The graph will exhibit the velocity of expansion by tracking how fast the colors are changing over time.

Adding a vertical reference line to indicate some pricing changes, we can see the effect of the new pricing on churn. This is particularly good to see for a monthly or quarterly analysis as opposed to yearly. The effect can also be analyzed across different cohorts of customers.

Finally, it is important to render a different Engagement Triangle for each customer segment, based on the previously defined Precision Segmentation that we covered in Chapter 3; then visually one can really see how the health of the business evolves over time in each of the relevant segments.

The Engagement Triangle is a simple yet powerful tool to visualize how customers are engaged with the business and at the appropriate cadence (monthly, quarterly or yearly). It clearly shows if their engagement deepens or weakens over time. It also exhibits the acceleration (or in some cases the deceleration) of new customer acquisition and correlation between churn and changes in the business. The color-coded version also demonstrates if customers are buying more and more over time. The Engagement Triangle should be periodically refreshed to see how much progress the company is making with its customers.

The delightfulness journey

The mismatch between delight that is experienced and delight that is expected, across the entire lifecycle of interactions between the user and the product or service, can be measured accurately. The lifecycle of interactions is a succession of steps that start with the very first time the product is unpacked or the service is experienced (*Discovery*) all the way to after the very last time the product or service is used (*Disposal*).

This measurement is called the *Delightfulness Coefficient*. It accurately highlights where, in the full product interaction cycle, misalignments happen. It can also be tracked over time to see if corrective actions taken by the company delivered the expected positive impact on the coefficient and contribution to top-line growth.

After a person or an organization has made the decision to buy a product or a service, has been through the process of the first three alignments (A1 to A3) and has acquired the product, then begins a progression of six consecutive steps I call the *Delightfulness Journey*. The six steps are as follows:

STEP	DESCRIPTION
1	Discovery
2	Usage
3	Maintenance
4	Support
5	Upgrade
6	Disposal

Six-step Delightfulness Journey

Here are more details on each them:

- **DISCOVERY:** This is the "unpacking" experience, when the product is taken out of its box and literally unpacked. It is also the feeling when stepping into a restaurant for the first time or sitting in a brand-new car and driving it out of the dealership.

- **USAGE:** This is where typically most of the time and energy is spent, although there are exceptions. For example, if one never has a car accident, then the usage of the car insurance service never materializes, which is a good thing!

- **MAINTENANCE:** This is what it takes to keep a product or service working as expected. This could be polishing the leather upholstery of a sofa, keeping the software updated on my PC, or keeping me happy as a Lufthansa passenger by staying engaged with me and offering relevant discounts and perks for future trips.

- **SUPPORT:** When something goes wrong with the product, how does it get fixed? This could be as simple as calling the Ford dealership to check my battery and as complicated as urgently flying a team of highly qualified technicians to fix a malfunctioning Fanuc robot in a car assembly-line factory.

- **UPGRADE:** This describes the path to make an existing product or service better. It could also be to replace it. When I want to upgrade from coach to business on a flight to London, how does that process take place? Even my car improves without my involvement via software updates.

- **DISPOSAL:** This is when the product or service is no longer wanted or used, but it can also be when it's replaced. It can be as complicated as switching from PeopleSoft to SAP or as simple as throwing a plastic cup in the right recycling bin at Starbucks.

In most cases, these steps are relevant, but there are exceptions. Sometimes, they simply do not exist. For example, in the clothing business, there is no notion of an upgrade. I can't go back to Target and have my white shirt upgraded. Not surprisingly, though, clever entrepreneurs have started subscription clothing companies such as Stitch Fix for women and Trunk Club for men, delivering monthly boxes containing curated selections based on customer requirements, lifestyles and price points, defining a new clothing-as-a-service trend!

In the Delightfulness Coefficient calculation, a weight in percentage is defined for each of the six steps, based on the existence and relative importance of each step (reflecting the fact that these steps don't have the same relative importance). The sum of the weights is always equal to 100% by design.

For example, if you take Starbucks[9], Tesla or KFC (Kentucky Fried Chicken), the six weights might look like:

---

9   One part of Starbucks' customer engagement in Usage involves conspicuous cultivation. I will return to Starbucks because I know the language and how to order coffee there. I'll have a skinny vanilla triple grande soy latte. I'd have no idea how to order that at Peet's.

STEP	DESCRIPTION	STARBUCKS	TESLA	KFC
1	Discovery	5%	10%	10%
2	Usage	75%	65%	90%
3	Maintenance	0%	5%	0%
4	Support	15%	10%	0%
5	Upgrade	0%	10%	0%
6	Disposal	5%	0%	0%

Example of weights for various companies

Then, for each of these steps, we ask via phone calls or online surveys a simple question based on a Likert-type rating scale. For example, on support, we would ask: "If you think about your experience at Starbucks *only as it relates to customer support*, please rate your support experience from the following:

1. Very unhappy
2. Unhappy
3. Somewhat unhappy
4. Somewhat happy
5. Happy
6. Very happy

For each of the six steps, we attribute a number based on the answer: -3 for very unhappy, -2 for unhappy, -1 for somewhat unhappy, +1 for somewhat happy, +2 for happy, and +3 for very happy. We then multiply the weight of each step by the average numbers generated by the answers. Finally, we normalize it so that the outcome is a number between -100 and +100. We call this final number the Delightfulness Coefficient.

Here is an example of the results for a company Blue Dots worked with:

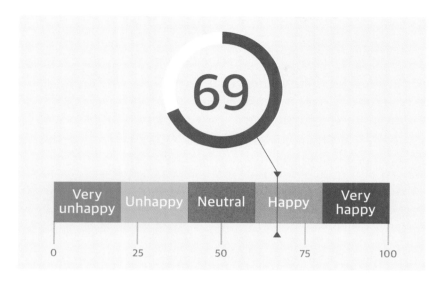

Example of Delightfulness Coefficient

This coefficient is critical because it measures the impending mismatch between the delight that is expected by the average user and the experience delivered by the company. In some cases, it is important to segment the user population, from the least impactful customers to the most impactful customers, in terms of potential and future contribution to revenue growth.

What is interesting is to measure that coefficient over time and address the negative areas to improve the Delightfulness Journey. Every business will want its Delightfulness Coefficient to go up over time and be as close as possible to 100.

Are you listening to your customers? Of course, you are!

How do we know if the customers' expectations are truly met?

Over my 28-year career, I have never met a CEO who has admitted he or she does not listen to his or her customers. In fact, I often get a reaction of offense and defiance when I dare to ask the question, "Are you listening to your customers?" How can a CEO not listen to his or her customers? It is a little akin to asking a parent, "Do you want to be a good parent?" Of course, I do! My next question to the CEO is more revealing: "How exactly do you listen to you customers?" Again, it is a little like asking an adult the follow-up question: "What exactly do you do to be a good parent?"

The answer becomes quite interesting and sometimes unexpected.

For example, one CEO explained to me that they listen to their customers by traveling to Chicago for a sales call. I kindly pointed out that unless a person or a company has given money in exchange for goods or services, that person or company is a prospect, not a customer. The salesperson is trying to convince someone to buy, in other words he is selling, which is obviously an important part of his job. Over the years, as a venture capitalist, I had the opportunity to listen to 2,600 pitches from CEOs raising capital. On a regular basis, I would hear a CEO say, "We have 24 paying customers." I always chuckle when I hear that. It's an oxymoron. They would not be customers if they were not paying! So, I follow up with a point of irony: "How many non-paying customers do you have?"

I have also had CEOs tell me that they love to sit in on support calls. They can hear the complaints and observe how customer support representatives engage to find a good resolution that makes the customer happier at the end of the call. While this is indeed listening to a customer, it is a conversation that is happening in a specific context of problem solving. Don't get me wrong—I believe there is value in CEOs sitting in on these calls, but this is not broadly and proactively listening to customers.

What I am talking about is a CEO picking up the phone and calling a customer out of the blue. Imagine the following conversation: "Hello, Jack, this is Brian Roberts. I am the CEO of Comcast. I am calling from our headquarters office in Philadelphia. I know you have been using Comcast Xfinity for your internet access for three and a half years. If I may, I have a simple question to ask you: 'What can we, at Comcast, do to make your life better?'"

Imagine the CEO of Aetna calling a mother in Oklahoma: "Good morning, Mrs. Jones. This is Mark Bertolini. I am the CEO of Aetna and am calling from Hartford, Connecticut. How are you doing this morning? I am calling because you have been a customer of Aetna since June of last year and I wanted to ask you how we, at Aetna, can make your health insurance experience better."

Imagine Jim Umpleby, the CEO of Caterpillar, calling one of the construction companies in Helinski, Finland, that is using their earth-moving equipment for a large renovation project, or Mary Barra, the CEO of GM, calling one of their dealerships in Atlanta.

I often wish I would be on the receiving end of those CEO calls. If Timothy Sloan, the recently retired CEO of Wells Fargo, had phoned me, I would have had plenty to say. Recently, after calling the bank with a simple question, "What is the routing number for my checking account?", I was subjected to an almost 30-minute ordeal of listening to messages, navigating phone trees, being put on hold, being asked the same security questions repeatedly, and finally, after receiving the routing number, being asked if I wanted to participate in a two-minute survey about my experience with Wells Fargo. It was all I could do to maintain my composure.

On the flip side, I wish Tony Hsieh, CEO of Zappos, would call me so that I could sing the praises of his organization. Their support team is pleasant, efficient, fast and customer-centric.

As I was doing research for this book, I had the opportunity to sit down with Tim Eades, the CEO of vArmour, a security company based in Mountain View, California. During our discussion about listening to customers, Eades shared an interesting idea that he implemented. He invites one or two customers to make presentations during each of his board of directors meetings. They are happy to share their experience, and board members can ask questions and hear directly from them. I thought this was a very good idea.

It does not matter how big or small the company is, whether it is local or global, selling to small or large businesses, consumers or governments. It does not matter if the business model is subscription or a one-time transaction. I would argue that for any CEO, actively reaching out to customers with the goal of truly listening to them is a critical and enlightening endeavor they should religiously pursue. This next section will propose a simple, but disciplined and honest approach to truly listening to customers.

The quest for the customer's truth

The first step is to segment customers by their real impact on revenue and potential for growth. This is because the way the company interacts with customers can be tailored according to their segment. For a company that counted 500 customers last year and generated $9.1 million in sales, here's how various customer segments can be defined.

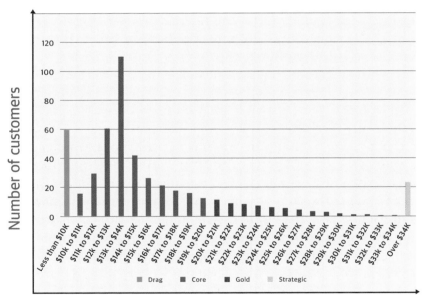

Customer distribution by annual revenue bucket

A close look enables us to sort the customers among four different types. Here is the breakdown:

TYPE	NUMBER	PERCENTAGE (of total number)	REVENUE (in $ millions)	KFC (of revenue)
Drag[10]	59	12%	$0.1	1%
Core	350	70%	$4.9	54%
Gold	67	13%	$1.6	18%
Strategic	24	5%	$2.4	27%
Total	500	100%	$9.0	100%

Customer distribution by type

In this example, the 59 Drag Customers represented 12% of all customers, but only contributed a mere 1% of total revenue. These customers can tend to be more demanding, although their net margin contribution is very low. A good strategy to deal with them is to gradually increase the price and trigger a natural churn over time, so that the number of Drag Customers can be significantly reduced without any serious impact on revenue (less than 1% in this example).

The Core Customers are the ones that fit the Ideal Customer Profile and represent what a typical "good" customer should be. At 70%, they constitute the vast majority of customers and contribute over half of total revenue. These are the ones that respond well to the basic product offering and should have the lowest churn rate.

10   Drag Customers are the customers that each generate a small amount of revenue ($10,000 in this example) and that all together contribute to a very small portion of total revenue (one percent in this example).

The Gold Customers are customers who spend more money with the company than the Core Customers. They may have started as Core Customers who used the product more and more and increased the amount of money spent with the company.

The Strategic Customers also spend a lot more than the Core. In this example, they outspend them by seven times. The company must develop a special, "white glove" relationship with them, as they have a large impact on the top line and can drive significant product improvement and enhancement. They need to be handled with a different approach than Gold Customers.

Here is a good approach to selecting which groups of customers to address. It starts by removing the outliers on each side: the Drag Customers and the ones who contributed a disproportionally large amount, the Strategic Customers. The CEO should have a deep relationship with all Strategic Customers and engage with them regularly to get to know them intimately.

Then, the CFO or the finance person randomly selects eight customers every month. For this whole exercise to be as statistically relevant as possible, it's important that the customers be randomly selected. Each week, the CEO follows the list and calls two customers, asking the simple question, "How can we, at My Company, make your life better at fill-in-the-blank?" Then the CEO should pause, carefully listen and take notes.

One important metric to track is the response velocity: how long did it take for that customer to respond to the call? It helps to have an assistant reach out to the customers initially by email and set up the call.

I can already hear the objection from CEOs: "Are you for real? Do you know how busy I am running a $360 million global company?" Each call should take approximately ten minutes and yield one or two takeaways from the customer's honest feedback. It could be as simple as "I am waiting too long in line at your store," or "I can't stand to wait 40 minutes on the support line because AT&T overcharged me." So, with two calls a week, 15 minutes for each call (10 minutes for the call plus 5 minutes typing the notes), at the end of each quarter, the CEO will have made 26 calls or 104 calls per year, spending about two hours a month. The results can then be tabulated using the following table:

NAME	CUSTOMER FOR	LEVEL OF HAPPINESS	WHAT I LEARNED
Michelle Dorian	2.5 years	4	Complained about product reliability.
John Didup	6 months	4	Wants access to more detailed product information.
Jackie Goldman	3 years	3	Product is too slow. Evaluating alternative solutions.

Examples of customer interview log

Note: The level of happiness is a scale from 1 = very unhappy to 5 = very happy. This does not measure the Delightfulness Coefficient as it is too simplistic, but it accomplishes a few things:

- Brings the CEO closer to the end customers and makes him or her more accountable for the customer experience.

- Delivers some direct, unedited feedback and suggestions on what to improve.

- Makes the CEO one of the very rare leaders who actually do listen to customers in an authentic, constructive and deliberate way.

- Allows the CEO to broadcast what was learned through the organization so changes and improvements can be tracked.

BLACKBERRY

Losing its fourth alignment

In March 1984, in Waterloo, Canada, Greek-Canadian business-man Mike Lazaridis and childhood friend Douglas Fregin formed a company named Research In Motion (RIM). It was the very first wire-less data development for commercial use in North America and the second company in the world, after Televerket in Sweden, to use the MobiText protocol. The company started by selling a number of wire-less solutions for vertical applications: a bar-code edge reader for motion picture film, a protocol converter, a point-of-sale terminal, a general-purpose MobiText X.25 gateway, radio modems and the RIM 900 two-way pager, which became the grandfather of the BlackBerry product line.

In 1997, RIM went public on the Toronto Stock Exchange under the symbol RIM and two years later, the company listed on the Nasdaq under the ticker BB. That year, the first RIM wireless email device was introduced using the BlackBerry Enterprise Server (BES) Software for Microsoft Exchange. This allowed RIM devices to send and receive emails. On March 4, 2002, the first device carrying the BlackBerry name was announced. It was the iconic BlackBerry 5810. It had a larger display and was also a phone that worked on a 2G network. It had a mini keyboard that so many of us fell in love with. At the time, the main RIM competitor was Palm. Competition started to heat up when the sleek Palm V came out.

If you look at RIM's revenue from 2004 to 2017 (the compa-ny's fiscal year ends on February 28), you will see an almost perfect Gaussian curve:

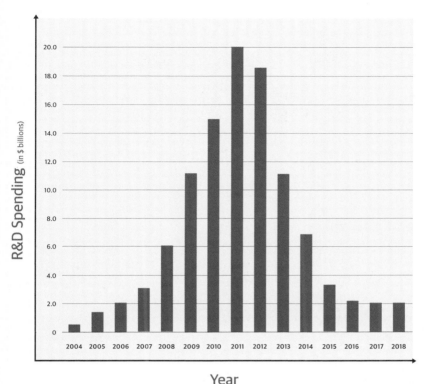

Year

RIM's annual revenue

Revenue peaked in 2011 at $19.9 billion. The iPhone was released in 2007 and kept persistently pushing innovation after innovation, setting up a solid pace that very few players, with the exception of Google with Android and Samsung, have followed. RIM doubled its R&D spending from $700 million in 2009 to $1.5 billion 2012, hoping it could keep up with the pace of innovation for smartphones, to no avail.

CASE STUDY

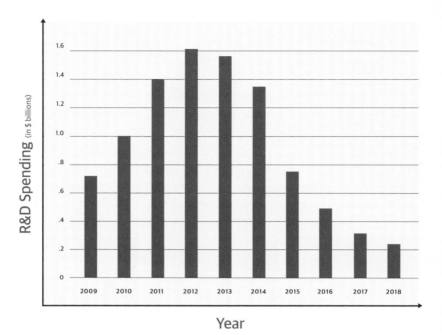

RIM's R&D annual spending

Ultimately, RIM's demise was because the company could not offer a better customer experience, from a marketing, sales, product and support standpoint, and effectively compete against Samsung and Apple. Not delivering the expected delight, the company lost its alignment along the A4 axis, pushing RIM to the state of low relevancy, where it lingers today.

CHEWY.COM

Sharing the love for pets

It was a cold morning in December when our mailperson delivered our mail. Like every weekday and Saturday, our dog, Rio, did not miss the opportunity to bark when he heard the familiar sound of our mailbox. Among the usual junk mail, invoices and reminders to make an appointment for our semiannual tooth cleaning was a nice blue envelope with a beautiful stamp, addressed to my wife. The address was handwritten in blue ink like a postcard coming from a friend. On the back of the envelope, in the same handwriting, it read: Chewy.com, 1855 Driffle Road, Suite B328, Dania Beach, FL 33004.

For these of us who have pets, Chewy.com is a familiar brand, all about healthy, balanced and quality food for our beloved companions. The company offers a variety of food, treats, toys and supplies for dogs, cats, birds, reptiles, other small pets and even horses. It also offers some good tips and advice on how to select the best diet for our pets. Chewy.com's website reflects their spirit with an upbeat style and a fair amount of enthusiasm:

> *Headquartered in Dania Beach, Florida (yes, we wear sandals all the time), Chewy.com's dedicated staff—furry and non-furry alike—are committed to providing the kind of service that makes you go "wow."*

The company was founded in September 2011 and raised a total of $451 million in equity and debt financing. In April 2017, less than six years later, PetSmart acquired the company for a whopping $3.35 billion. It became the largest eCommerce acquisition ever (bigger than the $3.3 billion Jet.com acquisition by Walmart announced in August 2016). Chewy reported sales of $3.5 billion in 2018, an increase of 67% from a year earlier. On June 14, 2019, Chewy.com raised more than $1 billion on its public offering and was valued at $14 billion at the end of the day.

In 2016, Chewy.com registered nearly $900 million in revenue, with spectacular growth. That growth was, in my opinion, driven by an obsessive A4 alignment and a cult culture around unprecedented customer service, a large selection of curated products and efficient shipping based on judicious placement of warehouses at strategic locations. This is not too dissimilar to what Zappos did in the footwear industry.

Back to the letter from Chewy.com—here is how it read:

> *Dear Patricia,*
>
> *This is a special time of year to reflect on all the good things in our lives. And of course, that includes the love we share with our furry family. They warm our hearts and put smiles on our faces every day. We're honored and grateful that you've trusted us to help keep their bellies full, and their days filled with joy, happiness and health.*
>
> *We wish you and your family the warmest wishes for the holidays and a very wonderful and happy New Year.*
>
> *Ryan Cohen and Michael Day*
> *Co-Founders*

After reading it, my wife came to me and said, "Look, this is a company that really cares about me." Truth be told, very few companies deeply establish such an emotional connection with their customers. Chewy does it in an elegant, smart and effective way. My only humble suggestion would be to reach out in the middle of the year, out of nowhere, to avoid being lost in the sea of sometimes unauthentic holiday wishes we receive from many other brands.

WHAT WE HAVE LEARNED

➤ The fourth axis of alignment is Delight ⟷ Offering. It's all about matching the expected delight with reality.

➤ The key of that alignment is to clearly define and control the *expected* delight. Once a product has been purchased, just before the very first time it is used, the customer has a certain expectation of what that product will do. It is critical that the actual experience meets that expectation.

➤ Missing the A4 Alignment triggers churn and disgruntled customers.

➤ The A4 alignment is measured by the *Delightfulness Coefficient*, and the results offer clues on how to remedy any issues.

➤ The difference between the received delight and the expected delight will dictate how much growth contribution will be realized in the future. If it is negative, there will be an adverse effect on the top-line growth. Conversely, if the difference is positive, then word-of-mouth will contribute to revenue growth.

CASE STUDIES

➤ BlackBerry: Losing its fourth alignment

➤ Chewy.com: Sharing the love for pets

NEXT CHAPTER

➤ Details why a data-driven approach is necessary and how alignment is precisely measured across the four axes in order the build the Growth Playbook.

"

Someday is not a day of the week.

DENISE BRENNAN-NELSON
author

CHAPTER

8

BUILDING YOUR GROWTH PLAYBOOK

I'm a doctor, not a psychic

Imagine a doctor in the emergency room who looks at a patient and must make life-and-death decisions, but she doesn't have any data. She does not know any of the four vital signs: blood pressure, heart rate, respiratory rate and body temperature. She can't triage and determine if urgent care must be administered. Knowing the vital signs is indeed critical. That's why they are called "vital." If you wake up with abdominal pain, you go to the hospital and the doctor doesn't do any tests, doesn't even examine your abdomen, yet declares, "You are suffering from appendicitis," as a patient, what would your reaction be? How much confidence would you place in this doctor's diagnosis? For me, the answer would be none.

Too many CEOs, executives, board members, investors, advisors and consultants sound like that ER doctor. Perhaps they are clairvoyant, but I'm not sure I would trust their judgment and decision-making. Daniel Kahneman, winner of the Nobel Prize in Economic Sciences, in his book *Thinking, Fast and Slow*, brilliantly addresses the temptation to make "gut" decisions that are not supported by facts. I found his approach on how our two systems with opposite speed work together to make decisions quite fascinating.

Alignment cannot be achieved without the right data, analysis and insights. Without measurement, it's like navigating using the direction of the sun or the stars compared to navigating with a GPS. When a doctor shows a patient an X-ray with a fine line on a bone and concludes that the patient has a fracture, it's hard to imagine that the patient will argue with the doctor's conclusion, the X-ray image, the equipment or the diagnosis. The real discussion should be around the options for treating the fracture. In many cases, a diagnosis can be addressed in more than one way. This is where the interaction with the doctor is most critical: weighing the pros and cons of various treatment approaches.

In business, as well, it's all about taking the emotions out of the decision-making process and replacing them with data, analysis and objectivity. This way, decisions are made with rigor, objectively and with less confrontation. I am certainly not opposed to intuition-based decisions, but there is an important caveat to it: they must be made with the clear recognition of the absence or lack of access to relevant data. **Data should always speak louder than opinions.**

Insights-based decision making

If data represent the dictionary of the words that are making the language of truth, then insights give the sense of what is expressed.

The world is awash in data. It's produced cheaply and exhaustively, every second. Think of smartphones. They have an array of sophisticated sensors and captors, such as ambient light sensors, accelerometers, barometers, fingerprint readers, GPS, gyroscope, magnetometers, proximity sensors, front and back cameras, and now 3D cameras for face recognition. They generate a lot of data relevant to where you are, who you are and what you are doing. According to Domo's Data Never Sleeps 5.0 report, released in June 2017, 2.5 quintillion (which is 2.5 billion billions or 2.5×10^{18}) bytes of data are generated every day in the digital sphere. By 2020, it is predicted that 1.7 MB of data will be created every second for every person on Earth. Data is generated, gathered, treated and stored at an insanely accelerated pace. The same Domo report indicates that 90% of all data was created in the last two years. The question is: what data really matters and how can insights be extracted from that mine of information?

Although decisions should be based on data, the absence of perfect data that leads to inescapable conclusions means people must make the best decision they can after analyzing the best data they can collect. Data is a foundation that, combined with intelligent creativity, enables making the right choices but, on its own, it is just data. How do good executives cross the chasm between data with insights and the creative solutions?

A good data-driven decision-making process starts with eight steps to generate the right data. The key is to not be swamped since so much data is available. This is why the best approach is to start by asking, "If we knew the answer to this particular question, would it make a difference in how we look at or think about the business challenges we face, and would it matter to our decision?" Deciding what question to answer, or framing the problem, is the fundamental starting point. It informs the first stage in the following eight-step circle process:

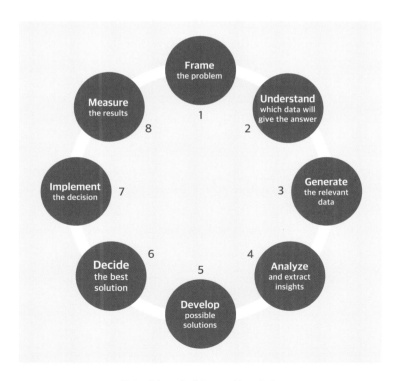

Data-driven decision-making circle

For example, if my business is to provide dog-walking or dog-sitting services to dog owners, there is a lot of information I can easily get, such as the average income my prospects have based on their area code. It wouldn't be helpful to know that 42% of them have blue eyes, because that doesn't affect my business whatsoever. However, if I find out that 52% of dog owners who are using my services have children in elementary school, I might tailor my marketing and services to this particular fact and play at an emotional level.

So, it's not about knowing everything about everyone and everything, it's about knowing a handful of key metrics that truly drive the business and then understanding the causality links that affect these key metrics. Nothing can be improved if it can't be measured. You need a baseline measurement and to follow the deviations from that baseline, positive or negative, to understand the impacts from decisions made.

Ideally, in any business, one should be able to have a simple dashboard with three to five top-key metrics to understand the health of the business. These are the vital signs of the company, using our ER analogy. On top of that, it's important to have a written plan, with commitment from the management team to measure and track deviations from the plan. Planning forces the business to make realistic assumptions that are believed to critically impact the business. Planning for goals and metrics should be done as a team exercise, once a year, with potential revisions after six months. This is the score sheet. It has to be integrated from product development to marketing activities, sales traction and customer success. The glue that holds it together is the budget allocation to execute the plan.

Every month, measurements are added to a chart tracking the vital signs to compare how things are progressing and understand deviations from the plan. The chart should include the original plan for the year, with any plan revisions, and the measured data. This approach helps track how close the business is to executing against the plan, within some guardrails.

Here is an example of actual revenue versus plan. Note that there are two plans: the one from last year and then a revised one that was proposed by the CEO and approved by the board in September:

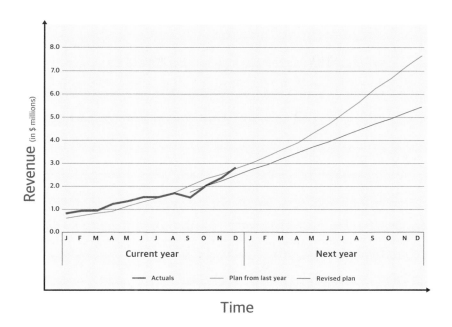

Revenue metrics tracking

It's important to identify the leading KPIs (key performance indicators) that signal the need for adjustment. This is where data, objectivity and insightfulness become critical.

Where does the data come from to measure alignment along the four axes?

 You can't lose weight if you don't step on the scale every day.

MUNJAL SHAH
CEO & co-founder of Health IQ

There are two types of data to examine: the data the company already has and new data generated for the purpose of extracting the right insights and informing the A4 alignment.

Data already created within the company can come from a variety of sources, such as:

- Financial systems: invoices, accounts receivable/accounts payable, asset ledger, payroll and compensation, etc.

- CRM systems, where marketing-qualified and sales-qualified leads are stored, deal stage velocity, attributes and correlations of closed/won and closed/lost, etc.

- Various customer touchpoints: site and page visits, log-in logs, store visits, purchase history, page abandonment history, close rate on special events or promotions, A/B testing results, click flow, customer support tickets, etc.

- Any other internal sources

One of the current trends is to link various data sources via a customer 360-centric view. It is part of customer success management, as we covered in the previous chapter.

Analyzing this data, understanding causality links and establishing precision segmentation will reveal critical insights that will help improve how customers are served and serviced.

The second type of data doesn't exist within the company. It comes from what's in the head of both internal and external stakeholders. Internal stakeholders include the CEO, members of the management team, board members, investors and advisors. External stakeholders comprise:

- Current customers

- Lost customers

- Current prospects

- Lost prospects

- Technology or IP partners

- Distributors, resellers, service providers, etc.

The art of asking the right questions

The way to generate external data is by directly approaching the right people and asking them the appropriate questions. This is done by conducting one-on-one phone interviews. I am not talking about an online survey asking for a Net Promoter Score (NPS) or some kind of Q-Score. This is not about asking someone to go to a website where the link is printed at the bottom of a receipt and answer a few questions. This is not a post-sales survey from a customer. I am somewhat skeptical about the methods and results of these types of surveys. Often, people answer to get a reward ("get a free Starbucks coffee if you answer these ten questions"), and because it's online, the survey is too rigid and you can't get a real feel of the emotional level about what is going on inside the head of the person. You lose the tone and emotion of voice, which carries 38% of the importance of the conversation[11].

I am talking about plain old phone conversations, conducted by someone who is not emotionally tied to the answer and has no vested interest whatsoever in the response, be it positive or negative.

I have used a well-defined process to conduct these external interviews and have done it more than 2,000 times over the course of 100-plus projects. The amount of insight that comes out of them is tremendous. In my view, it is critical for the interviews to be conducted by an outside firm because unbiased data is essential for getting to the truth. This impartiality ensures objectivity, integrity and honesty. I recommend working with a firm that has a lot of experience in conducting these kinds of phone surveys, as they can be tricky to execute.

There are some rules and a dash of art to asking the right questions and not getting carried away during the interview. It's a delicate balance between guiding the interviewees along the script and giving them some leeway to freely express their thoughts and ideas.

First off, people's attention span is very short. Preparation is essential so that you make every minute you have with the customer count. The questions have to be meticulously crafted and the flow carefully choreographed. There's no "winging it," and asking the wrong question can result in customers who feel their time has been wasted.

---

11   Source: combination of two research studies: Mehrabian & Wiener, 1967 and Mehrabian & Ferris, 1967.

There are many possible "right" questions one can ask, but here's one I find particularly revealing: "If I were to come on Friday afternoon and take away or unplug the product, how would you feel and how would you spend the weekend?"

Here's a good example of the wrong question to ask. Imagine that one of your customers has been using your product for a year and spends $1,990 per month for it on a subscription model with a one-year commitment. "Are you happy with the product?" would be the wrong question. The person made the decision to buy it and would have a hard time recognizing it was a mistake. I have never heard a customer say, "We spent $13,937 over the past seven months on this product and it's a bad product." This would be a confession that the customer made a mistake. Instead, the right questions to ask is, "What budget are you allocating for next year to that product? What about the following year?" This is quite interesting, because the number is a lot more telling. If the person does not want to continue using the product, you'll know from the number that is shared with you. The best answer is when the person is planning for a budget increase, which means that more usage of the product is anticipated and planned. Not only is this a vote of confidence in the product, but an increase in usage demonstrates stickiness in the organization.

From conversations to data that matters

Here is a description of the seven-step process I have been using and refining over the years for gathering and organizing the right data. This is an example for interviewing lost prospects. The primary goal is to understand truly and clearly why prospects made the decision to not buy and if the problem comes from a Claim versus Pain (A1) or a Message versus Perception (A2) misalignment.

STEP 1: LIST EXTRACTION

The process starts with downloading the CRM data from whatever tool the company is using, such as Salesforce, SugarCRM, HubSpot or any other tool. Then the list of all lost prospects in a given period of time—for example, over the past 18 months—is extracted. For consumer products that are not purchased directly from the company, that data needs to come from external sources, which can be expensive or not readily available.

STEP 2: SEGMENTATION

The lost prospect list is segmented based on particular attributes relevant to the business. As I covered in Chapter 5, this is an important step that relies on a good definition of the segmentation framework. For example, for a company selling to other businesses, it could be the size of those businesses based on number of employees, the industry they are in, the geographic distribution or other relevant products they bought. For companies selling to consumers, segmenting can be based on demographics or certain purchasing behaviors. There are always a few prospects that for one reason or another are an anomaly. These are the outliers and need to be excluded. If the goal is to conduct 40 interviews, the list needs to be much larger, likely 100 to several hundred lost prospects. Then, depending on the situation, approximately 80 customers are randomly selected from the list to account for those who will not respond to the interview request. Note that the random selection is critical in order for the results to be statistically relevant. If not done properly, the results could be biased and misguiding.

STEP 3: INTERVIEW GUIDE DEVELOPMENT

The interview guide is carefully crafted. The most effective interviews ask about a dozen questions and the majority of them are multiple choice. A few questions can be open-ended. The open-ended questions are the most difficult to analyze, and this is where building a taxonomy of keywords and some attributes for these keywords (for example: is it a positive or negative sentiment?) based on the answers is important for a correct and rigorous analysis. For a lost prospect survey, in the end, only one question is relevant: "Can you candidly share with me why you decided not to buy XYZ's product?" Most of the other questions are really to prepare for the question above and to make the person feel at ease. Start with some neutral questions to put people at ease, such as "How did you hear about XYZ?" or "Can you tell me your role and responsibilities at your company?" Sometimes, it makes sense to ask a question where you already know the answer, just to calibrate whether the person is forthcoming. An example would be "How much budget did you spend last year with XYZ?"

Of course, the company already has that information. Additionally, I like to finish the interview with some unexpected open-ended questions, such as "Is there any question I did not ask that I should have asked?"

One of the temptations when crafting the interview guide is to ask too many questions. It is very common for the CEO or a member of the management team to say, "Since we have the customers on the phone, why don't we ask if …" Often, the question does not really lead to any insights or actionable information. I call that the "Blue Eyes with a Cat" syndrome. It is a little bit like asking the interviewee on the phone, "Do you have blue eyes, and do you have a cat?" The answer is irrelevant.

It may seem counterintuitive, but we approach the development of the interview guide in the reverse order. Here is how it works. We ask ourselves, "If we knew that 78% of a particular group of respondents would give that particular answer, what would we learn about the business that we don't know now and why/how would it matter?" As I explained earlier in this chapter, we start backwards: we want to understand what insights are really relevant and impactful to the business and then we craft the key questions to get an answer. In other words, it starts from two basic questions: "What problem are we trying to solve?" and "What information do we need to know to be informed about that particular problem?"

Here is an example of an interview guide we recently developed at Blue Dots. Note that the company name ScaleRev, Inc. is fictitious.

Lost Prospect **Interview Guide**

INTERVIEWEE NAME: _____

INTERVIEWEE COMPANY: _____

INTERVIEWER: _____

DATE: _____

LOCATION: *By phone*

Introduction

Hello. As you know, my firm, Blue Dots Partners, has been retained by ScaleRev to better understand your experience as a prospective ScaleRev customer. We know how busy you are and appreciate you taking the time to share your insights.

Questionnaire

General and organizational

1. What is your current title at (COMPANY)? _____

2. What are your responsibilities and role there? _____

3. How many employees does your company have? _____

Interview sandbox

4. How much direct-to-consumer eCommerce volume does your company do in terms of number of transactions and revenue? If none, how much do you anticipate doing this year and next? _____

5. How much of your total revenue does direct-to-consume eCommerce represent? _____

6. How did you hear about ScaleRev? _____

7. How were you managing your eCommerce business prior to considering ScaleRev? Were you using another eCommerce services provider? If so, which one? _____

Decision making process

8. Why did you make the decision to NOT buy ScaleRev?_____
   _____

9. Did you instead purchase another eCommerce services provider? If so, which one?_____

10. Can you describe the pain that the solution you use today addresses for you?
    _____

11. How would you rate that pain (from 1 to 5)?
    1. Very low
    2. Low
    3. Neutral
    4. High
    5. Very high

12. What other solutions did you evaluate and why didn't you buy them?
    _____

13. How satisfied are you with the solution you use today (rate from 1 to 5)?
    1. Very low
    2. Low
    3. Neutral
    4. High
    5. Very high

Conclusion

14. What other comments would you like to make about ScaleRev?_____
    _____

15. Are there any questions I did not ask but should have asked?_____
    _____

I want to thank you very much for your great input and your time!

Interview guide example

STEP 4: EMAIL CAMPAIGN

We draft an email that the CEO will send to the targeted lost prospect list. One critical thing we insist on is that this is *not* a sales call. The goal is to get their honest feedback and ask for their views on how we could improve the business. Here is an example template of an email sent by John Doe, the CEO of ScaleRev:

Subject: Looking for your candid opinion

Hello Jack,

I hope you are doing well.

We are working with an experienced Silicon Valley-based management consulting firm called Blue Dots Partners to help us evaluate how we can better serve our customers.

I would really appreciate it if you could spend 20 minutes or so on the phone with them to share your completely candid feedback on our Partner Network program as well as any suggestions you might have to help us improve.

May I connect you with Philippe Bouissou, a Managing Partner at Blue Dots? He will work with you to schedule the interview for a time that conveniently fits into your busy schedule.

Thank you so much, Jack. We value your opinions and look forward to finding ways to better serve you and support your success.

Best regards,

John Doe

John Doe
CEO of ScaleRev, Inc.

Example of email sent by the CEO

STEP 5: CONDUCTING THE INTERVIEWS

After calendaring the interview, the phone conversation takes place. It typically lasts 20 to 30 minutes. The disadvantage of doing it by phone is that we miss the visual clues expressed through body language. The advantage, however, is that we can take notes directly on the computer by filling up the interview guide and capture the tone and emotion of the voice. It is important to share these notes with the company. In some cases, the interviewee might not be comfortable sharing his/her views. In that case, we redact the notes to respect the wish of the interviewee. However, the comment or opinion is taken into account in the final analysis.

STEP 6: SENDING A THANK-YOU NOTE

Remember to always send a nice and heartfelt thank-you note to the interviewees, telling them how much you appreciate them sharing their honest feedback and that it is valuable to the company.

STEP 7: TABULATING THE ANSWERS

The tabulation of the answers is done on Excel using what I call a Rows First, Columns Second approach. Here is the way it works: each column represents one of the questions asked and each row represents one of the interviewee's answers. If, for example, we asked 15 questions and interviewed 40 people, then we would have 16 columns, the first one being the name of the person, and 41 rows, the first one being the header row with the questions. We summarize the answer in each of the $40 \times 15 = 600$ cells. Once all the answers are entered, i.e. the rows are filled, then the analysis, column by column, can start, hence the name, Rows First, Columns Second.

Measuring alignment along each of the four axes

With the goal of conducting a number of phone interviews in a statistically relevant manner, the set of questions will vary depending on the axis and the specifics of the business. It is clear that a consumer buying a $49 wireless headphone and a large bank buying an anti-fraud subscription for over $1 million per year are not going to be preoccupied by the same challenges.

Here is some guidance and a set of questions to ask prospects/customers and the company in order to measure and analyze the gaps between the two sides, for each of the four axes:

PAIN

A1

CLAIM

**FROM THE CUSTOMER
POINT OF VIEW**

**FROM THE BUSINESS
POINT OF VIEW**

- What is pain? Where does it come from? How do you describe/articulate it?
- How painful is it? What is the intensity?
- How urgent to solve?
- What expectations do you have to solve the pain?
- Do you currently have a coping mechanism?
- What would you do if the product did not exist? (Current customers only)

**Gap
Analysis**
←——→

- What is the pain you are addressing?
- What is the main claim you are making?
- What are the secondary claims?
- Why are they unique and defensible?
- How do you demonstrate your claims? What proof do you have?
- Does the value outweigh the costs?

A1 Alignment questions

PERCEPTION

A2

MESSAGE

**FROM THE CUSTOMER
POINT OF VIEW**

**FROM THE BUSINESS
POINT OF VIEW**

- Market precision segmentation framework
- MECE segmentation taxonomy
- Size and growth rates for each relevant segment
- Pain level in each segment (heat map)
- Message understanding and receptiveness
- Competitive message responsiveness
- Competitive ecosystem

**Gap
Analysis**
←——→

- Existing market segmentation analysis
- Messaging segmentation
- Prioritization
- How are the target segments being identified and reached?
- Message for each targeted segment
- How do you generate demand?
- What is your strategic marketing?
- How do you broadcast your message?
  - ➤ PR, analysts
  - ➤ Key industry influencers
  - ➤ Social / digital marketing
  - ➤ Others...

A2 Alignment questions

PURCHASE	A3	SALE

FROM THE CUSTOMER POINT OF VIEW

- What is the go-to-market?
- Channel / distribution?
- Product / service acquisition mechanisms
- What are you buying?
- Can you resell? (if applicable)
- Payment terms
- Legal contract / Terms and Conditions
- Delivery timing
- How was your transaction experience? (SWOT analysis)
- Returns / defective product handling

Gap Analysis ◄─────►

FROM THE BUSINESS POINT OF VIEW

- Existing delivery mechanism
- Mapping with market segmentation
- What are you selling?
- Sales / distribution model
  - ➤ Direct
  - ➤ OEM
  - ➤ VAR
  - ➤ IP licensing
  - ➤ Other…

A3 Alignment questions

DELIGHT	A4	OFFERING

FROM THE CUSTOMER POINT OF VIEW

- The "delight" journey
- How is the total experience throughout the complete 6-step usage lifecycle?
- Measure importance and satisfaction level for the 6-step User Experience Journey
- Delightfulness Coefficient™ measure
- Virality mechanism: would you / did you recommend? Why? Why not?

Gap Analysis ◄─────►

FROM THE BUSINESS POINT OF VIEW

- Expected experience
- Relative importance of the 6 usage steps
- Tracking and KPI measurement
- Feedback mechanism (internal and external)
- Mapping with various market segments

A4 Alignment questions

To emphasize, what is important is to ask the right and pertinent questions. They have to be unbiased and relevant. They are very much context sensitive based on the type of product or service sold, the attributes of the prospects (based on the right segmentation), the mechanism by which the product is sold and the price/terms for the transaction.

The other important aspect to note is that the first three axes are concerning prospects, i.e. candidates to buy, not customers. The prospect becomes a customer only if and when the transaction takes place. So, for the first three axes, it is very important to assess both lost prospects, i.e. the ones who decided not to buy, and customers. Customers were prospects before making the decision to buy, so they were aligned along the first three axes, otherwise they would not have bought. I call them the Won Prospects.

From data to insights

Once the data is tabulated, then the analysis can take place. This is where critical insights are extracted and correlations established based on the appropriate segmentation.

Here is an example of measuring alignment along the A3 axis.

This is a question we formulated for a Blue Dots client, an $80 million software company selling to enterprises, to evaluate their customers' buying experience. We wanted to correlate it with each sales rep to benchmark them and understand how they could improve the buying experience. We conducted a series of 48 interviews with customers and one of the questions we asked was, "What adjectives would you use to describe your buying experience?" Each response was classified as positive (in blue) or negative (in orange). Here is a breakdown of the 87 answers we collected during our phone conversations:

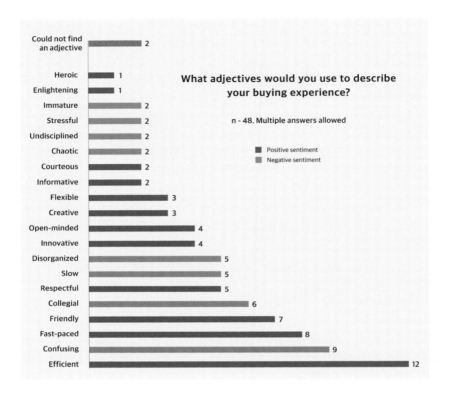

Could not find an adjective	2
Heroic	1
Enlightening	1
Immature	2
Stressful	2
Undisciplined	2
Chaotic	2
Courteous	2
Informative	2
Flexible	3
Creative	3
Open-minded	4
Innovative	4
Disorganized	5
Slow	5
Respectful	5
Collegial	6
Friendly	7
Fast-paced	8
Confusing	9
Efficient	12

What adjectives would you use to describe your buying experience?

n - 48. Multiple answers allowed

■ Positive sentiment
■ Negative sentiment

Example of responses

What did we learn from the customer feedback? First off, two respondents were not able to describe their buying experience with pure adjectives. The question was designed to elicit a spontaneous answer, but this question was clearly not something that these two respondents had strong feelings about, nor did their buying experience impact them in a major way either positively or negatively. On average, the other respondents shared 1.8 adjectives with us to describe their experience, which means that they had a relatively well-defined conception about it. Then, 68% of the responses were positive and 32% negative (highlighting some areas for improvement). It's interesting to note that none of the responses were neutral. So, if we had to calculate an alignment coefficient from zero to five just based on that question, it would be 3.4.

Based on the results, what corrective action did we recommend our client take? The big takeaway was that the sales reps are efficient, respectful and friendly with prospects. Overall, the sales organization was doing well. There were some cases where the experience was confusing, disorganized and somewhat undisciplined/chaotic. A more detailed analysis regarding the sales reps for those particular customers enabled the organization to improve the sales process and retrain or let go some of the reps. This later resulted in better engagements with prospects and overall improvement to the sales experience for both the company and its customers. It was reflected in an uptick in bookings generated by the newly trained salesforce and ultimately a 9% increase in the top line.

Measuring the BAS (*Business Alignment Score™*)

For the four axes of alignment, analyzing the responses informs us about the match between the prospect or customer's view and the company's own views. Based on statistical keyword analyses and weighting each response (positive, negative or neutral), a coefficient of alignment can be calculated and normalized from 0 (total misalignment) to 5 (perfect alignment) along each of the four axes. This is the way revenue growth is instrumented and can be measured. Once the four measurements are done, we end up with a web diagram that looks like this:

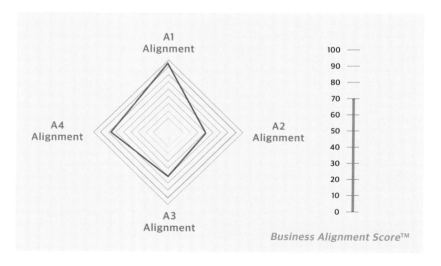

Measuring alignment

The *Business Alignment Score*™ (BAS) describes how well the business is aligned with its target market. A perfect alignment would be 100%. It is based on the measure of alignment between 0 and 5 for each of the four axes and calculated by dividing the blue area by the total area, which is 50.

The measurement of alignment with the method above is a snapshot of the current state of the business. What is important is to measure it and visualize how it evolves over time. Here is an example for an analysis conducted every quarter for two years:

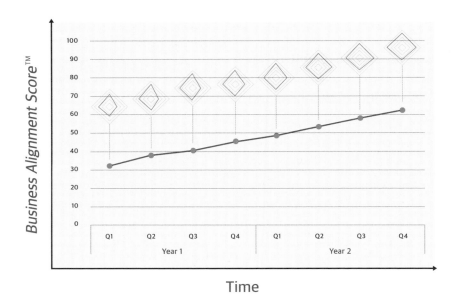

Tracking the BAS over time

Separating the "spatial" interrogation (the current alignment) with "temporal" information (the evolution of that particular alignment over time) is important. The latter is critical to measure to determine if the program implemented is successfully improving. The methodology has to be executed carefully to make sure that the sample for each survey is taken from the same market segment and that the randomly selected population is large enough. This is why both precision segmentation and random selection are so important.

Developing the Growth Playbook

For each of the four axes, calculating the alignment coefficient and the BAS will reveal where misalignments occur. Remember that there are two points that can be moved to rectify a misalignment: the prospect or customer's view and expectations, or the company's own position.

The customer's perspective can be changed either by shifting the expectation or by focusing on a different segment that is made up of prospects who are better aligned with the company's point of view.

The company's point of view can be changed by developing a new plan, executing it and measuring alignment against it to see if the plan delivered the expected results.

Based on this fundamental understanding of the misalignments, here is the process to develop the Growth Playbook:

1. Establish and prioritize a set of concrete actions to address the specific misalignments unearthed by the rigorous data analysis and insights discovered. This is the Growth Playbook.

2. Check that the plan is truly actionable: can the CEO and management team realistically execute it in a reasonable time frame?

3. Be specific in the execution including timeline, milestones, budget, and required headcounts with roles and responsibilities.

4. Can results be measured? The metrics to determine the success of the plan have to be established before the plan is implemented. There should be a process for periodic measurements if key metrics and early warning indicators show deviation. These are the "guardrails" for the company. Ultimately, the two key metrics that count will be the TAC and the impact on top-line revenue growth.

The Growth Playbook is a detailed plan for realignment along the four axes. It produces a successful outcome if and only if all of the following three criteria are met:

- **INSIGHTFUL:** What did we learn from the data analysis and alignment measurement that we did not know before?

- **ACTIONABLE:** Can the plan be implemented within the *Feasibility Envelope*? (See next section for details on this concept.)

- **IMPACTFUL:** What measurable difference did the plan make to our business? Did it matter? Did it move the top-line growth needle? How did the results tangibly translate into shareholder value creation?

Understanding the Feasibility Envelope

Having a plan is easy. Having a well-formed, data-driven and sound plan is hard. **Having a well-formed, data-driven and sound plan that can be executed is imperative.** Any growth action plan has to fit into what I call the Feasibility Envelope and has to be executable. In the end, execution of a good plan within the Feasibility Envelope is what truly matters. It's the art of the possible.

Not taking into account the Feasibility Envelope is a little like asking a short basketball player to train hard for the NBA. Over the past decade, with a few notable exceptions, very few players have been successful in professional basketball without being tall. It might seem unfair, but size actually matters a great deal in many sports, and asking a five-foot-five-inch person to put his heart and soul into the dream of playing for the NBA is both unrealistic and unreasonable.

What if a company decides to implement a new channel development program when no one on the sales team has ever dealt with channels and the company has no intention of hiring that expertise? What good would it be to recommend that a company buy one of their competitors when they don't have enough cash to execute the transaction and are not in a position to raise the funds? What good would it be to ask a company to change their product so much that it would be at odds with their core value?

One has to understand the sandbox, the space where new plans and ideas can realistically and reasonably take place. A number of parameters have to be considered, such as the proficiency of the management team, the ability to adopt and embrace change, budget considerations, the time horizon, and the ability to execute and follow the growth plan. In addition, there are often parameters that specifically depend on the company itself, its unique culture and DNA. While the Growth Playbook is based on aligning with the outside world (prospects and customers), it should never be crafted outside the Feasibility Envelope, otherwise it is destined to fail.

Four examples of Growth Playbooks and results

Here are four examples, one for each of the four axes, from clients we have worked with at Blue Dots:

A1 PAIN ⟷ CLAIM
ALIGNMENT PLAYBOOK AND RESULTS

CONTEXT

Client was an international B2B software company with a recurring SaaS business model, losing revenue momentum.

DATA ANALYSIS

Reviewed key business metrics, studied 84 months of invoicing history, defined a relevant customer segmentation framework and applied our Engagement Triangle tool.

INSIGHTS

Realized that the pace of new client acquisition was good, but there was no real growth in average monthly bookings and a devastating churn rate with 70% of customers lost in seven years, representing 57% of total billing. We conducted a series of lost customer interviews and realized that Pain and Claim were misaligned for certain customer segments. We then found out that lost customers had some common attributes—a signature. We designated them the Red customers and used the signature to characterize them.

GROWTH PLAYBOOK

We studied the current pipeline and realized that 40% of the prospects in the pipeline carried the same Red signature. We took these prospects out of the pipeline and asked the sales team to stop selling to them. Conversely, we were able to define a different set of characteristics for the Green customers, the ones who were loyal over a long period of time and had a much better Pain ↔ Claim alignment. We used that insight to redefine the Green prospects. We instructed the lead generation team to qualify only leads with the Green signature to provide the salesforce with a much better pipeline of highly qualified prospects.

RESULTS

In Q1 2016, we implemented a detailed lead generation program exclusively focused on Green prospects, with rigorous pipeline management. That year the company delivered its best year ever in its 14-year history. During the two following years, the company generated record revenue, with much higher morale in the lead generation and sales teams.

A2 PERCEPTION ⟷ MESSAGE ALIGNMENT PLAYBOOK AND RESULTS

CONTEXT

Company was selling outsourced low-cost leads for the banking industry.

DATA ANALYSIS

Analyzed a broad array of business data: financials, customers touch-points, competitive metrics. We interviewed 75 customers and developed a MECE competition segmentation of all customers.

INSIGHTS

We discovered that the problem was a misalignment between the Perception and Message. It turned out that the value proposition was not inexpensive leads, but the speed and volume at which quality leads were delivered. In other words, it was not lower cost, it was faster speed.

GROWTH PLAYBOOK

We retooled the message around a new expression of the Claim centered on sales acceleration, not lower cost. We built a brand architecture pyramid with the company logo on the top, and various layers going down the pyramid: the company name, the brand essence, the positioning, the brand personality and the foundation or base—the reasons to believe in the brand. Based on this brand strategy, we developed new marketing and sales support material, and launched a new website with customer testimonial videos.

RESULTS

The lead-to-sale time was improved by 52% for our Client, with the new disciplined sales culture that we fostered. The company achieved its best results the second quarter after implementation and was closing multiple six-digit deals in less than three quarters. The new value perception spurred an 18% increase in revenue, since the new time-to-market claim had a much higher resonance with prospects.

A3 PURCHASE ⟷ SALE
ALIGNMENT PLAYBOOK AND RESULTS

CONTEXT

Company was selling a popular service to 12 million consumers over the Web through three large partners.

DATA ANALYSIS

Analyzed key business attributes driving customer acquisition via these indirect channels. We mapped the competitive landscape, precisely measured the customer acquisition cost at an average of $48.06, established a new customer segmentation and evaluated an alternative partner ecosystem that would yield a 23% conversion rate.

INSIGHTS

We learned that the largest partner threatened to pull the plug on the entire market, which would have triggered a stunning loss of 55% of annual revenue. That partner indeed stopped its activity in the space just a year later. We needed to act fast as we anticipated the dramatic shift.

GROWTH PLAYBOOK

We decided to sell via new channel partners with complementary services targeting the same end prospects. We recrafted the value proposition to accommodate this new channel strategy with a redefined product offering supported by flexible fee-based packages. We built a new partner-driven business model to generate a five-times-per-customer revenue increase.

RESULTS

We reversed a looming loss of 55% of the top-line revenue to a 16% growth. The company generated additional revenue of $32.5 million based on the new business model. Consequently, the company strengthened its category leadership position, yielding significant shareholder value creation.

A4 DELIGHT ⟷ OFFERING ALIGNMENT PLAYBOOK AND RESULTS

CONTEXT

Enterprise software company suffering a substantial revenue growth decline that started in 2012.

DATA ANALYSIS

Conducted 90 current and past customer interviews, ran deep analysis of the customer retention cycle and evaluated the level of perceived delight through the entire product consumption.

INSIGHTS

A careful analysis of the interviews revealed that the expected delight versus what the customers received was grossly misaligned. We also realized the company wasn't focusing on managing and growing revenue within the existing customer base. Sales compensation was rewarding hunters, not farmers, and revenue growth suffered because of the loss of too many unhappy customers that were discovered too late.

GROWTH PLAYBOOK

We developed an early-warning system based on behavior signals that predicted a calculated probability of churn. We crafted and implemented an action plan for high-risk customers as well as structured account planning and retention programs. We aligned sales compensation to support a "no churn" policy and established metrics for installed based growth.

RESULTS

After implementation, customer retention was the highest ever in the history of the company, with almost no churn during the two years following execution of the new program. Within 90 days, installed-based revenue grew 35% quarter-over-quarter by focusing on existing customers' needs and opportunities. The fundamental issue was lack of care, not so much the product offering. By changing the expectation, the results were substantial. It would have been a lot harder, in terms of timing and costs, to change the product.

CASE STUDY

WHAT WE HAVE LEARNED

➤ Insights and action plan cannot be put together without first and foremost an objective, disciplined data analysis.

➤ Data comes from a combination of many signals captured from internal systems and a series of statistically relevant one-on-one phone interviews.

➤ The art of asking the right question must be applied to extract honest, true and meaningful insights. Relevant questions are crafted for each of the four axes of alignment, specific to the company's market and offering and for each relevant segment.

➤ Alignment along each of the four axes is measured on a scale from 0 to 5. From them, the BAS (*Business Alignment Score*™) can be calculated from 0% to 100%.

➤ Once misalignments are measured and understood, a Growth Playbook within the Feasibility Envelope can be crafted based on the misalignment insights discovered.

➤ Execution of the plan and measurement of top-line growth can then be applied.

➤ Four case studies illustrate how this new approach was implemented for four clients at Blue Dots.

CASE STUDIES

➤ Four examples of alignment playbook success from Blue Dots

NEXT CHAPTER

➤ Covers the criticality of internal alignment and execution.

"

Vision without execution
is just hallucination.

THOMAS EDISON
inventor

INTERNAL ALIGNMENT

Internal alignment makes growth happen. It is absolutely critical, as a perfect plan badly executed is a futile exercise. There are many outstanding books on aligning organizations for success as well as the critical functions that make up the organization, including marketing, sales, business development, customer care and more. My intention is not to dive deep in these areas, which explains why this chapter is fairly short. I do, however, want to highlight some of the key success factors for internal alignment and illustrate why it is essential to growth.

The magic of the Catching Organization

Some organizations never seem to be on top of things. You see employees running around with their hair on fire. No doubt, that's a sign of internal misalignment. Roles, responsibilities and tasks are unclear. I call these the *Catching Organizations*. The idea of the term came from a blog authored by Seth Godin that was posted on July 5, 2018. Godin is one of the world's best marketers and a prolific writer who has authored over 7,000 daily posts reaching more than a million readers, as well as 18 bestselling books in 36 languages. In his July 5, 2018 blog post, Godin's enlightening text reads like this:

Seven years ago, I shared a secret about juggling:

> *Throwing is more important than catching. If you're good at throwing, the catching takes care of itself. Emergency response is overrated compared to emergency avoidance.*

> *It's as true as it ever was, and it's not just about juggling. In fact, it's hardly about juggling.*

> *We spend most of our time in catching mode. In dealing with the incoming. Putting out fires. Going to meetings that were called by other people. Reacting to whoever is shouting the loudest.*

> *But if we learn a lesson from jugglers, we realize that the hard part isn't catching, it's throwing. Learn to throw, to initiate, to do with care and you'll need to spend far less time worrying about catching in the first place.*

Internal alignment changes organizations from Catching Organizations to Throwing Organizations. It enables the execution of the external alignment, i.e. the magic dance of the balls for the juggler.

Let's just fire the CEO

Before being in management consulting, I was a partner at Allegis Capital, an early-stage VC firm founded by Bob Ackerman and based in the heart of Silicon Valley, with $500 million under management. The firm was capitalized by 33 large corporations that were our limited partners and provided the capital we invested. It was an impressive list of multinational, mega-billion-dollar companies including AT&T, Best Buy, Boeing, Comcast, Fujitsu, General Electric, Hearst, J.P. Morgan, Mattel, Motorola, NBC, Procter & Gamble, Siemens, Société Générale, Telecom Italia and WPP.

I remember one day, walking into a board meeting for one of our portfolio companies. The CEO was clearly uncomfortable, as he had to explain why he missed his sales target by 18% for the quarter that just ended. An instinctive reaction to that situation is what I characterize as the self-defeating blaming circle. The notion is to quickly put the burden on sales. So, the CEO asked his VP of worldwide sales to present to the board and the VP defended his upsetting results by citing the lack of quality of the leads, which led to much lower-than-expected conversion rates. The VP of marketing then came in and complained that the product did not have all the features and functionality that were required to satisfy the particular market segments the company was targeting. When the head of product stood up, he explained that no one gave him the right product roadmap and the exact specifications of what customers really wanted, so he and his team built what they thought had the best feature set.

You get the picture: the Board meeting was a circus of finger pointing.

Unfortunately, this scenario happens all too frequently in board-rooms, the perfect symptom of internal misalignment. It is very hard to shoot at your companions-in-arms if all the weapons are pointing in the same direction (i.e., the hill the company is trying to conquer) as opposed to shooting in all directions, therefore at each other.

When I meet with VC or PE firms, I often hear this opening statement from the partner I am meeting with: "All of our portfolio companies are doing really well, growing fast, and we don't need your help." I remind them that I was a VC for close to a decade and I know that somewhere between 30% to 60% of their portfolio companies are not growing as fast as they would like, and are indeed suffering from various forms of growth trouble. Early-stage VC funds in particular will have a large number of casualties, as seed and early-stage investing is a risky business with inherently uncertain outcomes. It's the home run, that one big winner, that makes a fund. Two home runs and you are a top VC fund like Accel, Andreessen Horowitz, Benchmark, Greylock, Lowercase Capital, Sequoia, Union Square Ventures and others.

Then comes the second salvo from the VC partner: "If one of our portfolio companies is not growing as fast as we expect, we fire the CEO." While firing the CEO is at times the right, reasonable and legitimate decision, we do not believe that it's the right approach to solving the growth problem, and here's why:

1. It creates all kinds of unintended consequences, including significant disruption to the rest of the organization.

2. It does not answer the question "Why aren't we growing as fast as we'd like?" Growth could have stalled because of an A2 misalignment: the message is not aligned with the perception. In that case, the

person responsible might be the VP of marketing. Of course, ultimately, the buck stops at the CEO's desk, but the problem in this case can be addressed by means other than firing the CEO.

3. It takes at least four to six months to find a new CEO, then another three months or so for the new CEO to get his or her bearings and start to deeply understand why growth has stalled. In the end, it may take one year to get to the bottom of it and start fixing the real misalignment issues. This is way too long.

I would argue that if the core issue is slow revenue growth, then approaching the problem along the four independent axes is a much more effective, pragmatic and disciplined approach than bringing in a new CEO. It also has the advantage of initially keeping people, emotion and subjective thinking out of the equation and focusing on data and rigorous analysis.

How best to align all functions within an organization so that execution can be effective and successful? This is mainly driven by two critical factors: solid leadership that drives a strong culture along with a clear mission.

It all starts with solid leadership driving a strong culture

The first critical ingredient of internal alignment is leadership. Many books, ideas, opinions and points of view expound on the topic of leadership, so I won't attempt to tackle the subject here. But here is, in my opinion and in the context of alignment, what matters the most: a CEO, who leads the company, establishes a strong culture via a deliberate process and makes sure that everyone in the company is in lockstep and aligned behind the POV, the mission and the purpose. Maintaining these two related alignments is a large part of the CEO's job and responsibility. How is it done? By carefully hiring the right people with both the right character and competencies.

Every employee should be able to recite the company's mission without hesitation and with a strong sense of belonging and honest conviction about the culture. That mission must be truly believed and lived. It can't be fake. Like in music, it is the immutable score that everyone plays from. While every player has a different role in an orchestra, everybody is following the same score that dictates the key signature, the tempo and the dynamics.

Working in concert doesn't detract from the specialized talents or skill set of each individual. An oboe player is obviously trained differently than a percussionist or a viola player. However, players have the freedom to express, to a certain degree, their creativity through the exercise of their talent within the boundaries of the written score.

True leaders make sure that everyone understands his or her particular role. Only then will all players create magic in the music. Creativity from each is never sacrificed in the name of the mission, but in the end, harmony for a company will not happen without a strong culture and POV, just like in an orchestra. The best CEOs understand the need for internal alignment that starts by recruiting, trusting, training, delegating to and retaining the best players.

Merriam-Webster defines culture as "the set of shared attitudes, values, goals, and practices that characterizes an institution or organization." Culture always starts from the top, with a CEO who sets it and demonstrates it every day, every moment. Late management guru Peter Drucker stated that "culture eats strategy for breakfast." He was so right.

Organizations with a strong culture shine and win. Take the example of Lori Bush, former president and CEO of Rodan + Fields. During her eight-year tenure, she took the company from eight to over 300 employees and from relaunch in 2008 into its first $1 billion revenue year. In May of 2018, roughly two years following Bush's retirement, TPG bought 25% of the company at an estimated $4 billion valuation. As of publication, the company continues to be the number-one skin-care brand in North America.

When I spoke to Bush in January 2019, she explained that her philosophy was to always put the company's customers and independent representatives first, with "integrity beyond reproach." She and her team worked crazy hours and felt they were all on a mission. During the early years, Bush identified five specific core values that she called the True Colors (a nod to the five colors incorporated in the company's logo):

1. Assurance
2. Business savvy
3. Collaboration
4. Innovation
5. Transparency

Bush is convinced that the value she created during her tenure at Rodan + Fields could not have happened without this strong set of values and principles. In a way, it was the score of the symphony that she so masterfully conducted.

A strong culture helps companies cope with adversity and creates differentiation. It helps the organization deal with changes and flex its power at the right time, when necessary. Building a successful company that grows over long periods of time is tough, but in the end, it's about employees rallying behind the mission and caring about each other like a family. Ray Dalio magnificently shares some of his unorthodox approach to building a real culture in his book *Principles*, techniques he applied successfully at Bridgewater.

Another example of strong business value is Apple. I felt it very much when I worked there and it continues today. On an earnings call on January 21, 2009, Tim Cook explained:

We believe that we are on the face of the Earth to make great products and that's not changing.

We are constantly focusing on innovating.

We believe in the simple, not the complex.

We believe that we need to own and control the primary technologies behind the products that we make, and participate only in markets where we can make a significant contribution.

We believe in saying no to thousands of projects, so that we can really focus on the few that are truly important and meaningful to us.

We believe in deep collaboration and cross-pollination of our groups, which allow us to innovate in a way that others cannot.

And frankly, we don't settle for anything less than excellence in every group in the company, and we have the self-honesty to admit when we're wrong and the courage to change.

And I think regardless of who is in what job those values are so embedded in this company that Apple will do extremely well.

This is one of the most well-conceived, well-expressed and convincing points of view I have read.

The mission

Amir Rubin has an impressive background. He was the COO of UCLA Health for six years, then president and CEO of Stanford Health Care for five years, where he grew revenue from $1 billion to $3.5 billion and increased profits from $100 million to $500 million. He then moved to Optum (part of UnitedHealth Group), where he was EVP and divisional CEO for two years before becoming the CEO of One Medical Group. One Medical Group is on a mission to fundamentally transform health care for all, with a modern approach to primary care where living rooms are the waiting rooms, patients call doctors by their first names, and technology enables digital and virtual care. Their Net Promoter Score is an impressive 90%. One Medical Group has a DTC (direct-to-consumer) model where they charge $15 per month to the patient and then bill the patient's insurance directly for the care. More than 3,500 partner companies offer the service to their employees as a benefit, including Levy's, Google, Uber, PwC and many others. They are now the largest independent primary care provider in the US, with 1,300 employees and $200 million in revenue, and they are growing organically at 35% to 40% per year.

Rubin believes that, to best address the challenge of revenue growth, a company has to be oriented for growth. It cannot simply be growth for the sake of growth. The company must be mission-driven and guided by a purpose that everyone in the company can rally behind. The mission at One Medical Group is *Exceptional primary care, designed for real life,* and it animates everything Rubin and his team does.

This level of mission-driven passion starts with the founders. Take the example of Cyan Banister, a partner at Founders Fund, who was lifted out of poverty by capitalism. She dropped out of high school and was homeless and abhorred corporations. Her journey started when she received one paycheck and turned it into a successful business. She invested in the seed round that Uber raised at a pre-money valuation of $4 million, as well as other incredible moonshot projects such as SpaceX and Postmates. In a Term Sheet article published on October 18, 2018, she was asked by

Polina Marinova how she picked such early-stage companies. Here was her response:

> There's this narrative that people will tell you when they're trying to raise money. I look at the narrative and I look at the person, and I try to figure out first and foremost—does the narrative fit the person? You can tell whether it's a person who has found some sort of market niche that they're just trying to exploit, and they're pretending to be passionate. Those are the people I don't think are going to win. And then there are the people who think about it day and night and look in the mirror and dream about this thing they're trying to solve.

An entrepreneur's true character, vision and passion have to be aligned with the dream to build a real company. This is where the DNA of Category Leaders companies comes from.

That passion and dream become the magnetic north that aligns all compasses for the entire organization. It inspires. It lifts. It gives a purpose. It fuels the good vibes and the energy. It defines principles. It informs decisions. It invites the right set of actions and the right attitude. Without it, forces are not aligned and can cancel each other out. The mission compass tells everybody which direction to pull. It aligns everyone. As Jonathan Corr, the CEO of Ellie May, a Cloud-based technology company in the mortgage industry with over $500 million in revenue, shared with me: "Have a north star. Stick to it and pursue it relentlessly and get intimate with your customers along that journey."

Why internal alignment matters as much as external alignment

In the end, execution drives success and failure. Sustainable growth can't happen with poor implementation. It takes human beings working day in and day out to advance the cause of the company. Members of the organization make the claim possible, they carefully craft a clear yet powerful message, they insure the right method is in place to sell the product and they delight customers. People cannot be taken out of the total alignment equation. One can figure out the right strategy to accelerate and grow based on the four axes of alignment, but in itself the strategy is fruitless and futile without solid execution.

As Jai Das, president, managing director and co-founder at Sapphire Ventures, pointed out during a discussion I had with him as I was interviewing him for this book, "The secret of growth is the team." This is true at any stage of growth. The right team has a combination of left- and right-brain strengths. The collective right brain figures out the pain, the market and the wedge to attack that market. The collective left brain is focused on process and execution. People are the third pillar of success, along with product and sales. Only strong leadership that enables a robust culture driven by a powerful, authentic purpose will attract and retain the best possible talent.

Internal alignment is the process by which external alignment is executed. Various groups with different roles focus on the implementation along each of the four axes of alignment while other groups focus on providing the important and necessary supporting functions. Organizational design matters, as it is critical for a company to have the right structure and the right talent with the appropriate competencies, know-how and expertise.

Mark Rabe, the CEO of Sojern, a data-driven marketing company focused on the travel industry, grew the company from very little revenue to over $100 million in seven years. He spends a lot of time recruiting, engaging and retaining employees and setting them up for success. For Rabe, it's all about organization design, tools, platform and processes. He continually trains his employees. They have implemented something called the Quarterly Pulse to make sure everyone is on the same page. This coming year Rabe wants to recruit 175 new employees, and he has thought a lot about how to do it successfully. He knows it's important to understand group dynamics and how decisions are made collectively, as well as having the right management team that can truly scale the business.

One important dimension of the internal alignment is nimbleness and the ability of the organization to execute efficiently and react quickly, but sensitively, to market dynamics, especially in the field of technology. External alignment is not static, and the market changes sometimes at a high speed. In these situations, the key is to make micro-adjustments. Insights will come from these who are closest to customers, i.e. at the edge as opposed to in the boardrooms.

A good example of nimbleness and micro-adjustments is Amazon. They implement a number (200 or so) of small two-week "experiments." It doesn't cost much, and experiments that exhibit promising results get funded. The idea is to optimize the input variables, to generate significant growth contribution and reduce risk. The process is very decentralized. Each team is measured by improvement on the input variables. For example, it can be time to search or click rates, etc. This is how AWS (Amazon Web Services) was born (and IBM, Microsoft, SAP and others missed the cloud market initially). The finance team builds a model and determines if a real and positive contribution to growth can be realized. Everything is driven by long-term revenue. This approach resulted in Amazon's sponsored search results business growing from $700 million to $8.5 billion in two years, which is remarkable.

Executing the internal alignment

Once the growth playbook for the external alignment has been developed, then the organization is in charge of executing that alignment. It is imperative that it is fully aligned internally and that all groups work in harmony and support each other. There are eight axes of internal alignment or "internal gears." Each gear has its own role, function and purpose.

Eight axes of internal alignment

Here is how the eight functions map to the four axes of external alignment:

AXES OF ALIGNMENT	MAPPING TO A4 PRECISION ALIGNMENT™
Product Marketing / Product Development	Defines and develops the product to realize the claim (A1 alignment)
Marketing	Selects markets (precision segmentation), crafts messages and creates awareness (A2 alignment)
Business Development Sales, Go-To-Market, Sales Enablement, Sales Ops	Engineer the sales flywheel, i.e. the repeatable process to transform a prospect into a customer (A3 alignment)
Operations, Manufacturing Support	Enables manufacturing to work
Manufacturing	Builds the product and ships to the right place
Customer Care / Customer Success	Delivers delight (part of A4 alignment), makes sure that each customer finds success by using the product or the service
Finance, HR, Legal and IT	Supports the entire organization

Mapping the eight axes of internal alignment

Note that some companies might not have all eight of these functions. For example, a consulting organization or a law firm doesn't have manufacturing or operations support. Some of these functions are directly connected to the four external axes of alignment, some are support functions, but every group in an organization is a key contributor to manufacturing and delivering delight.

As a side note, I personally believe that the product marketing / product management team should be part of the product development team (as opposed to marketing), albeit separate. This is the team that determines the attributes, characteristics and expected performance of the product. They define what the product is supposed to achieve in order to deliver on the Claim.

The product marketing function is critically important. It directly interfaces with several other internal functions including product development, manufacturing, sales/go-to-market and customer care. They are the owners of the Claim.

SOUTHWEST AIRLINES

A magic internal alignment

On March 15, 1967, in Texas, Rollin King and Herb Kelleher founded a small airline called Air Southwest Co. The story goes that King explained the concept to Kelleher over dinner, by drawing a triangle on a napkin representing three cities: Dallas, Houston and San Antonio.

Shortly thereafter, a legal action was launched by some airline incumbents, most notably Aloha Airlines, United Airlines and Continental Airlines, to try and shut the young airline down. However, in December 1970, Air Southwest prevailed in a ruling by the Texas Supreme Court. It took three years and a great deal of tenacity for Kelleher to win that difficult legal battle.

Innovation was very much part of the early formative years at Southwest Airlines. The company pioneered the frequent-flyer mileage concept. One of its key hallmarks has always been its forward-thinking customer service. The company was the first in the airline industry to adopt an employee profit-sharing plan. It started in 1971 by giving 10% of the company ownership to its employees. That year, in March, the company changed its name to what it is now Southwest Airlines (LUV). Southwest began servicing the three Texas cities with its inaugural flight on June 18, 1971. The "Love Airline" was finally off the ground after a long and difficult labor.

In 1979, Cubic-Western Data self-ticketing machines were introduced in all airports where Southwest flew. Passengers could buy a ticket from the machine and go directly to the gate. Another hallmark of Southwest Airlines is its boarding policy that lets passengers choose their seats as they board the plane, while keeping a fair pecking order by groups. This boarding process continues to be applied today and is unique in the industry.

In 1973, the company generated its very first profit, and 1984 was the fourth consecutive year the airline was ranked number one in customer satisfaction. In 1998, Southwest Airlines became the fifth largest US carrier, flying more than 50 million passengers that year.

On the company's website, there is a quote from Gary Kelly, the current CEO of the airline, that says:

Our people are our single greatest strength
and most enduring long-term competitive advantage.

It is not about how many routes the company flies. It is not about how many countries it flies to or how many passengers it safely moves from point A to point B. It is all about the women and men who get up every day, do their jobs with enthusiasm and accomplish their mission to make people safe and happy, never losing their positive spirit. Kelly has always been a strong defendant of civility. He believes that employees need to treat each other like family and customers like guests. These attributes are definitely reflected in the company's mission:

Dedication to the highest quality of Customer Service
delivered with a sense of warmth, friendliness,
individual pride, and Company Spirit.

In June 18, 1976, Southwest celebrated its fifth anniversary and offered a banquet to all five-year employees. This was a true celebration of its culture and spirit.

Southwest has handsomely rewarded its shareholders. As of August 2017, it is the most valuable airline in the world, with $34 billion in market cap. The company generated $20.4 billion in sales in 2016 and grew its top line 3% from the previous year and 7% from 2014 to 2016. Its net income in 2016 was $2.2 billion. That year, it transported 152 million passengers. An analysis of the market capitalization per employee at the end of 2017, for the ten largest airlines in the world, shows that by far, Southwest generates the highest value per employee for its investors:

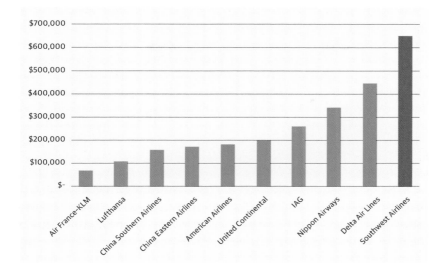

Airline valuation per employee

Southwest has managed to build success by staying true to itself and driving its growth plan with focus and passion. Its execution machine is well oiled, its employees are well trained and the culture has never been an afterthought. It is Southwest. The crew truly enjoys welcoming people onboard with a friendly and positive attitude. In March 2009, David Holmes became known as "The Rapping Flight Attendant" on a flight to Oklahoma City, by asking passengers to clap a beat so that he could deliver the welcome onboard and safety announcement by rapping. He started by saying, "These of you who have flown with us before know that we do things a little bit differently on Southwest," and he ended his rap song by concluding, "Thank you for my beat. I appreciate that. You will not see this on United. I guarantee."

Boy, is he right!

ZAPPOS

A zabulous story

Here is another case of great internal alignment.

In 1998, Nick Swinmurn was frustrated because he could not put his hands on a pair of brown Airwalks that fit him at his local mall in San Francisco. Some stores had the wrong color, others the wrong size. He came back home, disappointed, with no Airwalks. A few months later, he discussed with Tony Hsieh and Alfred Lin the idea of selling shoes online. Shortly thereafter, Shoesite.com was born. Inspired by the flexibility of the name Amazon, which didn't restrict Jeff Bezos from selling things other than books, the name of the company was quickly changed to Zappos. Interestingly, if you go to www.shoesite.com, you are automatically directed to guess what site? Yes, Zappos indeed! Imagine Amazon being initially called Booksite.com?

The name Zappos came from the Spanish word for shoes, zapatos. A second p was quickly added to make sure people would not pronounce it zay-pos, and the rest is pretty much history.

Today, Zappos has extended its business beyond footwear. The site offers bags and handbags, clothing, accessories, jewelry, watches, sunglasses, travel accessories and luggage. Just as Amazon quickly expanded from its initial target of books, Zappos extended its business outside its initial focus on shoes.

In January 2000, a letter arrived at the Zappos office. No, it was not a complaint, but a delighted customer who was singing the praises of the phone call she had just experienced with a Zappos representative. While the two pairs of shoes she was interested in were not available, the efficiency and kindness of the Zappos Customer Loyalty Team, plus the gift certificate and T-shirt that were sent to her for the inconvenience, really made an impression on her. The "Zappos way" was born.

In early 2005, Hsieh asked every single employee what the core values were at Zappos and distilled the 37 ideas he gathered into what is known now as the Ten Core Values. Here is what they are:

1. Deliver Wow Through Service

2. Embrace and Drive Change

3. Create Fun and a Little Weirdness

4. Be Adventurous, Creative, and Open-Minded

5. Pursue Growth and Learning

6. Build Open and Honest Relationships with Communication

7. Build a Positive Team and Family Spirit

8. Do More with Less

9. Be Passionate and Determined

10. Be Humble

In November 2009, in an unsurprising move given the natural fit, Amazon acquired Zappos for close to $900 million. Alignment between the two companies along shared goals and the relentless obsession for a delightful customer service sealed the marriage. In a smart move, Amazon agreed to let Hsieh run the company independently and keep its culture and way of engaging with customers intact.

In his email to all employees on July 22, 2009, Hsieh wrote:

Amazon focuses on low prices, vast selection and convenience to make their customers happy, while Zappos does it through developing relationships, creating personal emotional connections, and delivering high touch ("WOW") customer service.

The transaction was motivated by a strong belief from management and the board that it will accelerate the growth of the Zappos brand and help them fulfill their mission of delivering happiness faster. Indeed, growing and spreading happiness is the mission of the company.

Now headquartered in the former City Hall in downtown Las Vegas, the 1,500 Zappos employees work shoulder to shoulder to deliver the best customer experience and have demonstrated that a large and growing business can thrive almost entirely by nailing the A3 axis of alignment:

the alignment between the purchase process and the sales process via an easy, friendly and exciting way of product acquisition.

It's part of the company's DNA to put the customer front and center. In fact, if you visit Zappos, the entire office space is designed around the "heroes," the customer support agents. These are the heroes who don't mind spending time with customers to really listen and make them as happy as possible, the ones who are not scripted and can connect with customers with their own style and personality. Hsieh sits in the same-sized cubicle as everyone else, right in the middle of his team.

On June 11, 2016, Zappos customer support employee Steven Weinstein broke an unprecedented record and spent 10 hours, 43 minutes on a call. The call started with him helping a customer place an order, then expanded into a long chat covering all kinds of topics like vacations, restaurants and places they visited. Weinstein took only one break and his colleagues made sure he had water and food.

What's unique about Zappos is that the product is not the shoes, and it's not their eCommerce website. It is the emotional engagement, the service, the way customers are treated. It's the pre- and post-sales support. This is what Zappos is all about. Few companies truly understand the criticality of the A3 axis alignment in the alignment methodology. Zappos pushed it very far and that is, no doubt, the key reason for their success. Naturally, the amazing internal alignment made the execution of the external alignment possible. Rallied behind strong leadership, culture and mission, Zappos touches people's hearts at a breathtaking pace!

➤ Without internal alignment, no growth plan can be successfully executed. A plan without execution is futile.

➤ Internal alignment always starts with solid, passionate leadership that establishes and enforces a strong culture.

➤ Internal alignment is possible when it is supported by a mission, cause, point of view, belief and the conviction that defines why a company does what it does, beyond just creating value for its shareholders or making money.

➤ Executing the four axes of external alignment relies on internal alignment across eight key functions within the organization, acting as the internal gears of the complex corporate mechanism.

➤ Growing the top line faster than the market to drive unprecedented shareholder value creation will only happen if *both* external and internal alignments are realized.

CASE STUDIES

➤ Southwest Airlines: A magic internal alignment

➤ Zappos: A zabulous story

SUMMARY

The key to solving the growth puzzle

The concept of *A4 Precision Alignment*™ was born from years of collaborating with companies of all shapes and sizes on their growth challenges and strategies. It's a universal, rigorous, data-driven and prescriptive methodology to realize a perfect alignment between a company and the markets in which it operates. I won't fool you. It's not easy or trivial. It takes commitment and hard work to adopt and execute this methodology. But rarely do I meet a CEO who is daunted by hard work. It goes with the job. So my hope is that this book and the stories of companies that have succeeded—or gone off the rails—will inspire you to dig deeper and use these techniques to accelerate your business. I promise you, it will be worth it.

A4 Precision Alignment™ at a glance

For those of you who want a quick reference on the *A4 Precision Alignment*™ concepts or are one of those readers who skip to the end, here's a summary of the methodology.

A4 Precision Alignment™ is based on the existence of four universal and independent axes of alignment connecting eight dots between a business and its customers. That's it. Each of the four pairs of dots must be aligned. That's it. It applies to a café on the Left Bank in Paris, a startup company, a $10 million manufacturing business, a $150 million mid-market software company or the largest companies on Wall Street. Specifically, these four axes are: Pain versus Claim, Perception versus Message, Purchase versus Sale and Delight versus Offering.

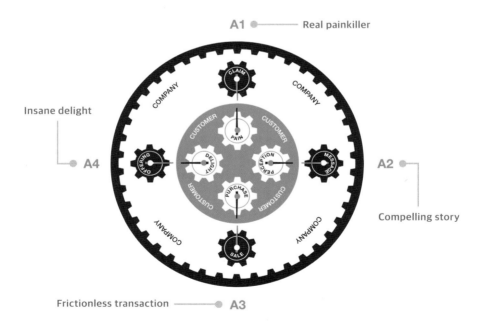

The four axes of alignment and eight dots to align

This new paradigm has been successfully tested and applied by many CEOs, general managers and business owners to an array of challenges in multiple industries, resulting in significant quarterly and yearly revenue growth. Some simply wanted to maintain their revenue momentum; others were suffering from aggressive competition and were forced to cross the growth chasm. Some were missing their sales plans; others had experienced a flattening top line and were chasing the next S-curve in the hopes of reigniting their growth engine.

The power of this transformative approach is in the fact that alignment along each of these four axes can be accurately measured on a scale from zero to five by a simple yet comprehensive methodology that illuminates the path of growth. This is done by capturing, measuring and analyzing mismatches between the prospect or customer's view and the company's own view, using the tools and techniques described in this book. The four measurements become the construct of a web diagram that looks like this:

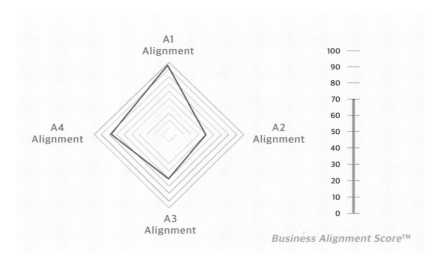

Measuring alignment

The *Business Alignment Score™* (BAS) describes how well the business is aligned with its market. A perfect alignment would be scoring at 100%.

Developing the Growth Playbook

These measurements reveal unique insights into areas of weakness that are the cause of misalignments and are responsible for slowing down the top line. These insights form the basis for developing a Growth Playbook, which is a concrete plan of action for the CEO and the management team. It provides a roadmap, a set of executable actions, all defined within the Feasibility Envelope. *Aligning the Dots* explains how to develop your Growth Playbook.

One of the key advantages of this new approach is that these four axes are independent from each other, meaning that one can take action to realign on one axis without introducing misalignment on any of the other three axes.

In order to execute the Growth Playbook, the organization must be aligned as well. Internal alignment is a different challenge that is addressed first by solid leadership that establishes and enforces a strong culture and second by a mission, a cause, a set of beliefs and inalterable convictions that define why a company does what it does beyond just creating value for its shareholders or making money.

The *A4 Precision Alignment*™ methodology is a new lens through which the challenge of revenue growth and relevant actions can be brought into focus. It demonstrates how the complex puzzle of alignment, which often eludes even the most experienced management teams, is solved by developing a clear blueprint, so that everyone knows what to do on Monday morning when the clock chimes eight.

INDEX

P

R

S

ACKNOWLEDGMENTS

I could not have written this book without the encouragement, support and constructive feedback from two persons I would like to recognize. Patricia, my loving wife, you have a beautiful heart and have been my life's person forever. I feel so lucky and blessed to have you. Also, my friend and business partner, John Orcutt, who has been by my side in the Blue Dots venture. John, your sense of humor, wit and experience have been, and continue to be, critical to our success. It is a blessing to work with you. Thank you both, from the bottom of my heart.

To my loving children, Sandra and Adrien: thank you for your support and advice throughout this journey.

Lori Bush, Don Hogle and Alain Ries: you have given me your most precious resource—your time. Each of you reviewed my very first manuscript with care and commitment and above all, with a sharp eye. You critiqued it with honesty and clarity. I took all your comments, suggestions and questions to heart and this book has been much improved because of each of you.

Karla Olson, you shepherded me through the process of writing, editing, designing, printing, publishing and launching this book, dealing gracefully with my questions, demands and time constraints. Elaine Cummings and Lisa Wolff, you spent dozens of hours editing the book, helping with the structure, flow and organizational aspects of the manuscript, all the way down to the most subtle punctuation rules I naively didn't know existed.

Charles McStravick, you did a terrific job designing the cover, the jacket and the inside of the book. Karla, Elaine, Lisa and Charles, your tastes and talent are truly amazing. I also want to thank you, Kate Purmal. Sharing your experience in writing *The Moonshot Effect* was invaluable to me. Your advice, suggestions and kindness have helped me at every step of the process. A big mahalo to you, Guy Kawasaki, for your advice on writing, launching and marketing *Aligning the Dots* and of course, for always smiling.

Finally, I had the honor of interviewing over 110 CEOs, investors, board members and entrepreneurs as I was doing research for this book. Each of you has helped me refine my concepts, ideas or models. I compiled this list with the caveat that I may have unintentionally forgotten someone, and if so, my sincere apologies. Thanks to each of you for your sharing your thoughts, experience and wisdom.

Keith Alper, Founder and CEO, Geniecast

Léo Apotheker, former CEO, SAP and HP

Shellye Archambeau, Board member, Verizon and Nordstrom,
former CEO of MetricStream

Rod Beckström, Founder and CEO, BECKSTROM

Eric Benhamou, Chairman and General Partner,
Benhamou Global Ventures, former Chairman and CEO, 3Com

Anne Bouverot, former CEO, Morpho

Herman Bulls, Vice Chairman, Americas,
JLL and Corporate Board Director

Dave Burke, CEO and Chairman, Makena Capital

Lori Bush, former President and CEO, Rodan + Fields

Nolan Bushnell, CEO, X2 Games, founder
and former CEO, Atari and Chuck E Cheese!

Pascal Cagni, Founder and CEO, C4 Ventures,
former General Manager, Apple Europe

Philippe Camus, Senior Advisor, Evercore

Augusto Cavalcanti, CEO, Daitan

Satjiv Chahil, former Chief Marketing Officer, Apple

Henry Chesbrough, Executive Director,
Center for Open Innovation, UC Berkeley

Randy Chesler, President and CEO, Glacier Bancorp

Bruce Chizen, former CEO, Adobe

Tarek Chouman, CEO, eFront

David Chung, Executive Director, HGGC

Steve Ciesinski, President, SRI International

Lynda Clarizio, former President, Nielsen US Media

Bruce Cleveland, Founding Partner, Wildcat Venture Partners

Gill Cogan, Partner, Opus Capital

Ryan Cohen, founder and former CEO, Chewy.com

Bill Coleman, former CEO, BEA

Ed Colligan, Managing Director, Edventures

Jonathan Corr, CEO, Ellie Mae

Bracken Darrell, CEO, Logitech

Jai Das, Managing Director, Sapphire Ventures

John Dean, President and CEO, Central Pacific Bank,
former Chairman and CEO, Silicon Valley Bank

Anand Deshpande, Founder and Chairman, Persistent Systems

Peter Dolan, Managing Director, Makena

Jeff Drazan, Managing Partner, Bertram Capital

Donna Dubinsky, CEO, Numenta

Mike Dulworth, President and CEO, Executive Networks

Phillip Dunkelberger, CEO, Nok Nok Labs

Eric Dunn, CEO, Quicken

Tim Eades, CEO, vArmour

Peter Economy, The Leadership Guy, Inc. Magazine

Bill Elmore, General Partner, Foundation Capital

Mike Farley, Chairman, Tile

Brad Feld, Managing Director, Foundry Group

Noel Fenton, Founding Partner, Trinity Ventures

Bob Finocchio, former CEO, Informix

Drue Freeman, CEO, ACG Silicon Valley

Misty Frost, CEO, Career Step

Jay Fulcher, Chairman and CEO, Zenefits

Jean-Louis Gassée, Venture Partner, AllegisCyber

Dan Gillmor, educator, author, columnist, speaker

Nacho Giraldo, Partner, TPG Growth

Ken Goldman, President, Hillspire

Dan Gordon, Chief Operating Officer, Gordon Biersch

Brian Grey, CEO, Remind.com

John Hennessy, Chairman, Alphabet

Ben Howe, CEO, AGC Partners

Cédric Hutchings, former CEO, Withings

David Hyman, CEO, Unagi Scooters

Brian Jacobs, Partner, Emergence

Brad Jones, Partner, Redpoint Ventures

Chris Keene, CEO, Gigster

Alan Kessler, former CEO, Thales e-Security

Chuck Kissner, Chairman of the Board, Rambus

Abe Kleinfeld, CEO, GridGain

René Lacerte, Founder and CEO, Bill.com

Ray Lane, Managing Partner, Greatpoint Ventures,
former President, Oracle Corporation,
former Chairman, Hewlett Packard and Carnegie Mellon University

Gerry Langeler, former President, Mentor Graphics

Cathy Lego, board member at Cypress Semiconductor,
IPG Photonics and Lam Research

Ken Levy, Founder and former CEO, KLA Tencor

Mitchell Levy, CEO, HappyAbout

Bernard Liautaud, Managing Partner, Balderton Capital

Carol Mills, board member at Zynga and RELX Group

Geoffrey Moore, author, speaker, advisor

Richard Moran, former CEO, Frost and Sullivan

Doug Murray, CEO, Big Switch

Chris Neil-Jones, Managing Partner, Talent Capital Partners

Mickey O'Neil, CEO and President, Silicon Valley Investment Group

Tim O'Reilly, CEO, O'Reilly Media

Amit Patel, CEO and President, Rakuten Americas

Dmitry Pushkarev, EIR, Kleiner Perkins

Mark Rabe, CEO, Sojern

M.R. Rangaswami, Managing Director, Sand Hill Group

Bill Reichert, Managing Director, Garage Technology Ventures

Cliff Reid, CEO, Travera

Heidi Roizen, Partner, Threshold Ventures

Alain Rossmann, former CEO, Phone.com

Odile Roujol, founder, Fab Ventures,
former CEO and President, Lancôme International (L'Oréal)

Amir Rubin, CEO, One Medical Group

Eric Salama, CEO, Kantar

Anita Sands, board member at ServiceNow, Symantec,
Pure Storage, ThoughtWorks

Paul Schaut, CEO, Aginity

Kathryn Schifferle, Founder and CEO, Work Truck Solutions

Greg Schott, CEO, MuleSoft

Gordon Segal, Founder and former CEO, Crate and Barrel

Munjal Shah, CEO, Health IQ

Claude Sheer, co-founder and Executive Chairman at Vizsafe

Chris Shipley, author, advisor

Mihir Shukla, CEO, Automation Anywhere

Rob Siegel, Partner, XSeed Capital

Leo Spiegel, Managing Partner, Mission Ventures

Lip-Bu Tan, CEO, Cadence, Chairman of Walden International

Reed Taussig, former CEO, ThreatMetrix

Armand Thiberge, CEO, SendinBlue

Christoph Tonini, CEO, Tamedia

Bill Trenchard, Partner, First Round Capital

Pete Ungaro, CEO, Cray

Ron Unkefer, Founder and former CEO, The Good Guys

Andy Vitus, Partner, Scale Venture Partners

Maynard Webb, Founder, Webb Investment Network,
board member at Salesforce, Visa, former Chairman of Yahoo

Ann Winblad, Managing Director, HWVP

Paul Witkay, Founder and CEO, Alliance of Chief Executives

Bob Wright, Managing Director, Firebrick Consulting

Chris Yeh, Co-author of Blitzscaling

Tony Zingale, former CEO, Clarify, Mercury Interactive
and Jive Software

Chris Zook, Author of Profit from the Core

Mitch Zuklie, CEO and Chairman, Orrick

ABOUT THE AUTHOR

Philippe Bouissou, Ph.D. has spent three decades in Silicon Valley as an entrepreneur, a CEO, a venture capitalist and a management consultant. He is Managing Partner at Blue Dots Partners LLC, a firm he co-founded focused on top-line acceleration. He started his career as the founder and CEO of G2i, Inc., a Unix software company that was acquired by Matra. He then was Senior Vice President at Matra Hachette Multimedia, Inc., where he led US business development for electronic publishing for the $12 billion, high-tech and diversified media company before joining Apple as Director of the Worldwide Internet Commerce group, where he founded and managed the online Apple Store and grew its revenue from zero to $350 million.

After Apple, Bouissou became a venture capitalist and successfully invested $43 million and generated double-digit cash-on-cash IRR. For over half a decade, Bouissou co-managed the Milestone Group, a management consulting firm serving over 220 clients. During his career, Bouissou led over 120 management-consulting projects with companies such as Cisco, Microsoft, SAP and Verisign and served on the board of directors of 20 companies, including ACG (Association for Corporate Growth) Silicon Valley, where he currently serves.

Bouissou graduated from École Normale Supérieure in Paris and holds a BS in Mathematics, an MS in Physics and a Ph.D. in non-linear physics and chaos theory.